ANALYTIC CULTURE IN THE US
INTELLIGENCE COMMUNITY

The Center *for the* Study *of* Intelligence

Central Intelligence Agency

Washington, DC 20505

Library of Congress Cataloguing-in-Publication data

Johnston, Rob

Analytic Culture in the US Intelligence Community: An Ethnographic Study/ Dr. Rob Johnston

Includes bibliographic references.

ISBN 1-929667-13-2 (pbk.:alk paper)

1. Intelligence—United States. 2. Intelligence analysis. 3. Intelligence policy. 4. Intelligence training.

Typeset in Times and Ariel.

Printed by Imaging and Publication Support, CIA.

Cover design: Imaging and Publication Support, CIA.

The pensive subject of the statue is Karl Ernst von Baer (1792–1876), the Prussian-Estonian pioneer of embryology, geography, ethnology, and physical anthropology (Jane M. Oppenheimer, Encyclopedia Brittanica*).*

ANALYTIC CULTURE IN THE US INTELLIGENCE COMMUNITY

AN ETHNOGRAPHIC STUDY

DR. ROB JOHNSTON

Center *for the* Study *of* Intelligence

Central Intelligence Agency

Washington, DC

2005

ACKNOWLEDGEMENTS

There are literally slightly more than 1,000 people to thank for their help in developing this work. Most of them I cannot name, for one reason or another, but my thanks go out to all of those who took the time to participate in this research project. Thank you for your trust. Particular thanks are due the other researchers who coauthored chapters: Judith Meister Johnston, J. Dexter Fletcher, and Stephen Konya.

There is a long list of individuals and institutions deserving of my gratitude, but, at the outset, for making this study possible, I would like to express my appreciation to Paul Johnson and Woody Kuhns, the chief and deputy chief of the Central Intelligence Agency's Center for the Study of Intelligence, and their staff for their support and to John Phillips and Tom Kennedy of the Intelligence Technology Innovation Center who, along with their staff, administer the Director of Central Intelligence Postdoctoral Fellowship Program.

I would like to thank Greg Treverton and Joe Hayes for their help throughout this project and for their willingness to give of their time. Dr. Forrest Frank, Charles Perrow, and Matthew Johnson deserve recognition for the material they contributed. Although it was not possible to cite them as references for those contributions, these are indicated in the footnotes, and I give them full credit for their work and efforts.

I would also like to thank Bruce Berkowitz, Mike Warner, Fritz Ermarth, Gordon Oehler, Jeffrey Cooper, Dave Kaplan, John Morrison, James Wirtz, Robyn Dawes, Chris Johnson, Marilyn Peterson, Drew Cukor, Dennis McBride, Paul Chatelier, Stephen Marrin, Randy Good, Brian Hearing, Phil Williams, Jonathan Clemente, Jim Wilson, Dennis, Kowal, Randy Murch, Gordie Boezer, Steve Holder, Joel Resnick, Mark Stout, Mike Vlahos, Mike Rigdon, Jim Silk, Karl Lowe, Kevin O'Connell, Dennis Gormley, Randy Pherson, Chris Andrew, Daniel Serfaty, Tom Armour, Gary Klein, Brian Moon, Richard Hackman, Charlie Kisner, Matt McKnight, Joe Rosen, Mike Yared, Jen Lucas, Dick Heuer, Robert Jervis, Pam Harbourne, Katie Dorr,

Dori Akerman, and, most particularly, my editors: Mike Schneider, Andy Vaart, and Barbara Pace. Special thanks are also due Adm. Dennis Blair, USN (Ret.), and Gen. Larry Welch, USAF (Ret.), and their staff.

There were 50 peer reviewers who made sure I did not go too far afield in my research and analysis. Again, there are mitigating reasons why I cannot thank them by name. Suffice it to say, their work and their time were invaluable, and I appreciate their efforts.

Because I cannot name specific individuals, I would like to thank the organizations of the Intelligence Community that gave me access to perform this research and made available research participants: Air Force Intelligence; Army Intelligence; Central Intelligence Agency; Defense Intelligence Agency; Department of Energy; Department of Homeland Security; Bureau of Intelligence and Research, Department of State; Department of the Treasury; Federal Bureau of Investigation; Marine Corps Intelligence; National Geospatial Intelligence Agency; National Reconnaissance Office; National Security Agency; Navy Intelligence.

Thanks are also due the following: Institute for Defense Analyses; the Sherman Kent Center and the Global Futures Partnership at the CIA University; the CIA's Publications Review Board; Office of Public Affairs, National Archives; Joint Military Intelligence College; Advanced Research and Development Activity, Defense Advanced Research Projects Agency (DARPA); International Association of Law Enforcement Intelligence Analysts; Drug Enforcement Administration and the DEA Academy; FBI Academy; National Military Intelligence Association; Association of Former Intelligence Officers; MITRE; RAND; Analytic Services, Inc. (ANSER); Potomac Institute; Center for Strategic and International Studies; Woodrow Wilson International Center; Booz Allen Hamilton; Naval Postgraduate School; Columbia University; Dartmouth College; University of Pittsburgh; Georgetown University; Carnegie Mellon University; Cambridge University; Johns Hopkins University and the Advanced Physics Laboratory; George Mason University; Harvard University; Yale University; American Anthropological Association; Society for the Anthropology of Work; Society for Applied Anthropology; National Association for the Practice of Anthropology; Inter-University Seminar on Armed Forces and Society; Royal Anthropological Institute, and the national laboratories.

I express my sincere apologies if I have failed to include any individuals or organizations to which thanks are due. Moreover, any errors of commission or omission are my own. God knows, with this much help, there is no one to blame but myself. Mostly, though, I would like to thank my long-suffering wife, to whom this book is dedicated. Thanks, Jude.

CONTENTS

Part IV: Notes on Methodology

FOREWORD

Gregory F. Treverton

It is a rare season when the intelligence story in the news concerns intelligence analysis, not secret operations abroad. The United States is having such a season as it debates whether intelligence failed in the run-up to both September 11 and the second Iraq war, and so Rob Johnston's wonderful book is perfectly timed to provide the back-story to those headlines. The CIA's Center for the Study of Intelligence is to be commended for having the good sense to find Johnston and the courage to support his work, even though his conclusions are not what many in the world of intelligence analysis would like to hear.

He reaches those conclusions through the careful procedures of an anthropologist—conducting literally hundreds of interviews and observing and participating in dozens of work groups in intelligence analysis—and so they cannot easily be dismissed as mere opinion, still less as the bitter mutterings of those who have lost out in the bureaucratic wars. His findings constitute not just a strong indictment of the way American intelligence performs analysis, but also, and happily, a guide for how to do better.

Johnston finds no baseline standard analytic method. Instead, the most common practice is to conduct limited brainstorming on the basis of previous analysis, thus producing a bias toward confirming earlier views. The validating of data is questionable—for instance, the Directorate of Operation's (DO) "cleaning" of spy reports doesn't permit testing of their validity—reinforcing the tendency to look for data that confirms, not refutes, prevailing hypotheses. The process is risk averse, with considerable managerial conservatism. There is much more emphasis on avoiding error than on imagining surprises. The analytic process is driven by current intelligence, especially the CIA's crown jewel analytic product, the *President's Daily Brief* (PDB), which might be caricatured as "CNN plus secrets." Johnston doesn't put it quite that way, but the Intelligence Community does more reporting than in-depth analysis.

None of the analytic agencies knows much about the analytic techniques of the others. In all, there tends to be much more emphasis on writing and communication skills than on analytic methods. Training is driven more by the druthers of individual analysts than by any strategic view of the agencies and what they need. Most training is on-the-job.

Johnston identifies the needs for analysis of at least three different types of consumers—cops, spies, and soldiers. The needs of those consumers produce at least three distinct types of intelligence—investigative or operational, strategic, and tactical.

The research suggests the need for serious study of analytic methods across all three, guided by professional methodologists. Analysts should have many more opportunities to do fieldwork abroad. They should also move much more often across the agency "stovepipes" they now inhabit. These movements would give them a richer sense for how other agencies do analysis.

Together, the analytic agencies should aim to create "communities of practice," with mentoring, analytic practice groups, and various kinds of on-line resources, including forums on methods and problem solving. These communities would be linked to a central repository of lessons learned, based on after-action post-mortems and more formal reviews of strategic intelligence products. These reviews should derive lessons for individuals and for teams and should look at roots of errors and failures. Oral and written histories would serve as other sources of wherewithal for lessons. These communities could also begin to reshape organizations, by rethinking organizational designs, developing more formal socialization programs, testing group configurations for effectiveness, and doing the same for management and leadership practices.

The agenda Johnston suggests is a daunting one, but it finds echoes in the work of small, innovative groups across the Intelligence Community—groups more tolerated than sponsored by agency leaders. With the challenge workforce demographics poses for the Community—the "gray-green" age distribution, which means that large numbers of new analysts will lack mentors as old hands retire—also comes the opportunity to refashion methods and organizations for doing intelligence analysis. When the finger-pointing in Washington subsides, and the time for serious change arrives, there will be no better place to start than with Rob Johnston's fine book.

INTRODUCTION

In August 2001, I accepted a Director of Central Intelligence postdoctoral research fellowship with the Center for the Study of Intelligence (CSI) at the Central Intelligence Agency. The purpose of the fellowship, which was to begin in September and last for two years, was to identify and describe conditions and variables that negatively affect intelligence analysis. During that time, I was to investigate analytic culture, methodology, error, and failure within the Intelligence Community using an applied anthropological methodology that would include interviews (thus far, there have been 489), direct and participant observation, and focus groups.

I began work on this project four days after the attack of 11 September, and its profound effect on the professionals in the Intelligence Community was clearly apparent. As a whole, the people I interviewed and observed were patriotic without pageantry or fanfare, intelligent, hard working, proud of their profession, and angry. They were angry about the attack and that the militant Islamic insurgency about which they had been warning policymakers for years had murdered close to 3,000 people in the United States itself. There was also a sense of guilt that the attack had happened on their watch and that they had not been able to stop it.

Having occurred under the dark shadow of that attack, this study has no comparable baseline against which its results could be tested, and it is difficult to identify biases that might exist in these data as a result of 11 September. In some ways, post-9/11 data may be questionable. For example, angry people may have an ax to grind or an agenda to push and may not give the most reliable interviews. Yet, in other ways, post-9/11 data may be more accurate. When people become angry enough, they tend to blurt out the truth—or, at least, their perception of the truth. The people I encountered were, in my judgment, very open and honest; and this, too, may be attributable to 9/11. In any case, that event is now part of the culture of the Intelligence Community, and that includes whatever consequences or biases resulted from it.

Background

The opportunity to do this research presented itself, at least in part, as a result of my participation in a multiyear research program on medical error and failure for the Defense Advanced Research Projects Agency (DARPA).[1] The DARPA research focused on team and individual error in minimally invasive or laparoscopic surgical procedures. This research revealed that individual errors were cognitive rather than purely psychomotor or skill-based. For example, some surgeons had trouble navigating three-dimensional anatomical space using the existing laparoscopic technology, with the result that these surgeons would identify anatomical structures incorrectly and perform a surgical procedure on the wrong body part.

Other individual errors were discovered during the DARPA studies, but, for the most part, these were spatial navigation and recognition problems for which there were technological solutions. Team errors, unlike individual errors, proved to be more challenging. The formal and informal hierarchical structures of operating rooms did not lend themselves to certain performance interventions. Generally, junior surgical staff and support personnel were not willing to confront a senior staff member who was committing, or was about to commit, an error.

The culture of the operating room, coupled with the social and career structure of the surgical profession, created barriers to certain kinds of communication. For a surgical resident to inform a senior surgeon in front of the entire operating room staff that he was about to cut the wrong organ could result in career "suicide." Such a confrontation could have been perceived by the senior surgeon as a form of mutiny against his authority and expertise and a challenge to the social order of the operating room. Although not universal, this taboo is much more common than surgeons would care to admit. Unlike individual errors, purely technological solutions were of little value in trying to solve team errors in a surgical environment.

The DARPA surgical research was followed up by a multiyear study of individual and team performance of astronauts at the National Aeronautics and Space Administration's (NASA) Johnson Space Center. Results of the NASA study, also sponsored by DARPA, were similar to the surgical study

---

[1] Rob Johnston, J. Dexter Fletcher and Sunil Bhoyrul, *The Use of Virtual Reality to Measure Surgical Skill Levels.*

with regard to team interactions. Although, on the face of it, teams of astronauts were composed of peers, a social distinction nevertheless existed between commander, pilots, and mission specialists.

As with surgery, there was a disincentive for one team member to confront or criticize another, even in the face of an impending error. Eighty percent of the current astronauts come from the military, which has very specific rules regarding confrontations, dissent, and criticism.[2] In addition to the similarities in behavior arising from their common backgrounds, the "criticism" taboo was continually reinforced throughout the astronaut's career. Virtually any negative comment on an astronaut's record was sufficient for him or her to be assigned to another crew, "washed out" of an upcoming mission and recycled through the training program, or, worse still, released from the space program altogether.

Taboos are social markers that prohibit specific behaviors in order to maintain and propagate an existing social structure. Generally, they are unwritten rules not available to outside observers. Insiders, however, almost always perceive them simply as the way things are done, the natural social order of the organization. To confront taboos is to confront the social structure of a culture or organization.

I mention the surgical and astronautical studies for a number of reasons. Each serves as background for the study of intelligence analysts. Astronauts and surgeons have very high performance standards and low error rates.[3] Both studies highlight other complex domains that are interested in improving their own professional performance. Both studies reveal the need to employ a variety of research methods to deal with complicated issues, and they suggest that there are lessons to be learned from other domains. Perhaps the most telling connection is that, because lives are at stake, surgeons and astronauts experience tremendous internal and external social pressure to avoid failure. The same often holds for intelligence analysts.

In addition, surgery and astronautics are highly selective and private disciplines. Although their work is not secret, both groups tend to be shielded from the outside world: surgeons for reasons of professional selection, training, and the fiscal realities of malpractice liability; astronauts because their community

---

[2] National Aeronautics and Space Administration, *Astronaut Fact Book*.

[3] NASA has launched missions with the shuttle fleet 113 times since 1981 and has experienced two catastrophic failures. It is probable that both of those were mechanical/engineering failures and not the result of astronaut error. Surgical reporting methods vary from hospital to hospital, and it is often difficult to determine the specific causes of morbidity and mortality. One longitudinal study of all surgical procedures in one medical center puts the surgical error rates at that center between 2.7 percent and 7.5 percent. See Hunter McGuire, Shelton Horsley, David Salter, et al., "Measuring and Managing Quality of Surgery: Statistical vs. Incidental Approaches."

is so small and the selection and training processes are so demanding.[4] Intelligence analysts share many of these organizational and professional circumstances.

The Intelligence Community is relatively small, highly selective, and largely shielded from public view. For its practitioners, intelligence work is a cognitively-demanding and high-risk profession that can lead to public policy that strengthens the nation or puts it at greater risk. Because the consequences of failure are so great, intelligence professionals continually feel significant internal and external pressure to avoid it. One consequence of this pressure is that there has been a long-standing bureaucratic resistance to putting in place a systematic program for improving analytical performance. According to 71 percent of the people I interviewed, however, that resistance has diminished significantly since September 2001.

It is not difficult to understand the historical resistance to implementing such a performance improvement program. Simply put, a program explicitly designed to improve human performance implies that human performance needs improving, an allegation that risks considerable political and institutional resistance. Not only does performance improvement imply that the system is not optimal, the necessary scrutiny of practice and performance would require examining sources and methods in detail throughout the Intelligence Community. Although this scrutiny would be wholly internal to the community, the concept runs counter to a culture of secrecy and compartmentalization.

The conflict between secrecy, a necessary condition for intelligence, and openness, a necessary condition for performance improvement, was a recurring theme I observed during this research. Any organization that requires secrecy to perform its duties will struggle with and often reject openness, even at the expense of efficacy. Despite this, and to their credit, a number of small groups within the Intelligence Community have tasked themselves with creating formal and informal ties with the nation's academic, non-profit, and industrial communities. In addition, there has been an appreciable increase in the use of alternative analyses and open-source materials.

These efforts alone may not be sufficient to alter the historical culture of secrecy, but they do reinforce the idea that the Intelligence Community itself has a responsibility to reconsider the relationship between secrecy, openness, and efficacy. This is especially true as it relates to the community's performance and the occurrence of errors and failure. External oversight and public debate will not solve these issues; the desire to improve the Intelligence Com-

---

[4] There are currently 109 active US astronauts and 36 management astronauts. See National Aeronautics and Space Administration-Johnson Space Center career astronaut biographies.

munity's performance needs to come from within. Once the determination has been found and the necessary policy guidelines put in place, it is incumbent upon the Intelligence Community to find and utilize the internal and external resources necessary to create a performance improvement infrastructure.

Scope

This project was designed explicitly as an applied research program. In many respects, it resembles an assessment of organizational needs and a gap analysis, in that it was intended to identify and describe conditions and variables that affect intelligence analysis and then to identify needs, specifications, and requirements for the development of tools, techniques, and procedures to reduce analytic error. Based on these findings, I was to make recommendations to improve analytic performance.

In previous human performance-related research conducted in the military, medical, and astronautic fields, I have found in place—especially in the military—a large social science literature, an elaborate training doctrine, and well-developed quantitative and qualitative research programs. In addition to research literature and programs, these three disciplines have substantial performance improvement programs. This was not the case with the Intelligence Community.

This is not to say that an intelligence literature does not exist but rather that the literature that does exist has been focused to a greater extent on case studies than on the actual process of intelligence analysis.[5] The vast majority of the available literature is about history, international relations, and political science. Texts that address analytic methodology do exist, and it is worth noting that there are quantitative studies, such as that by Robert Folker, that compare the effectiveness of different analytic methods for solving a given analytic problem. Folker's study demonstrates that objective, quantitative, and controlled research to determine the effectiveness of analytic methods is possible.[6]

The literature that deals with the process of intelligence analysis tends to be personal and idiosyncratic, reflecting an individualistic approach to problem solving. This is not surprising. The Intelligence Community is made up of a variety of disciplines, each with its own analytic methodology. The organizational assumption has been that, in a multidisciplinary environment, intelli-

---

[5] There are exceptions. See the appendix.
[6] MSgt. Robert D. Folker, *Intelligence Analysis in Theater Joint Intelligence Centers.* Folker's study contains a methodological flaw in that it does not describe one of the independent variables (intuitive method), leaving the dependent variable (test scores) in doubt.

gence analysts would use analytic methods and tools from their own domain in order to analyze and solve intelligence problems. When interdisciplinary problems have arisen, the organizational assumption has been that a variety of analytic methods would be employed, resulting in a "best fit" synthesis.

This individualistic approach to analysis has resulted in a great variety of analytic methods—I identified at least 160 in my research for this paper—but it has not led to the development of a standardized analytic doctrine. That is, there is no body of research across the Intelligence Community asserting that method X is the most effective method for solving case one and that method Y is the most effective method for solving case two.[7]

The utility of a standardized analytic doctrine is that it enables an organization to determine performance requirements, a standard level of institutional expertise, and individual performance metrics for the evaluation and development of new analytic methodologies.[8] Ultimately, without such an analytic baseline, one cannot assess the effectiveness of any new or proposed analytic method, tool, technology, reorganization, or intervention. Without standardized analytic doctrine, analysts are left to the rather slow and tedious process of trial and error throughout their careers.

Generally, in research literature, one finds a taxonomy, or matrix, of the variables that affect the object under study. Taxonomies help to standardize definitions and inform future research by establishing a research "road map." They point out areas of interest and research priorities and help researchers place their own research programs in context. In my search of the intelligence literature, I found no taxonomy of the variables that affect intelligence analysis.

Following the literature review, I undertook to develop working definitions and a taxonomy in order to systematize the research process. Readers will find the working definitions in the first chapter. The second chapter highlights the the broader findings and implications of this ethnographic study. Because the first two chapters contain many quotes from my interviews and workshops, they illustrate the tone and nature of the post-9/11 environment in which I worked.

The taxonomy that grew out of this work was first described in an article for the CSI journal, *Studies in Intelligence,* and is presented here as Chapter

---

[7] There is no single Intelligence Community basic analytic training program. There is, however, community use of advanced analytic courses at both the CIA University and the Joint Military Intelligence College. The Generic Intelligence Training Initiative is a recent attempt to standardize certain law enforcement intelligence analysis training programs through a basic law enforcement analyst training curriculum. The program has been developed by the Training Advisory Council, under the Counterdrug Intelligence Coordinating Group and the Justice Training Center.

[8] See the appendix.

Three. In addition to the normal journal review process, I circulated a draft of the taxonomy among 55 academics and intelligence professionals and incorporated their suggestions in a revised version that went to press. This is not to assert that the taxonomy is final; the utility of any taxonomy is that it can be revised and expanded as new research findings become available. The chapter by Dr. Judith Meister Johnston that follows offers an alternative model—more complex and possibly more accurate than the traditional intelligence cycle—for looking at the dynamics of the intelligence process, in effect the interrelationships of many elements of the taxonomy

The following chapters, prepared by me and other able colleagues, were developed around other variables in the taxonomy and offer suggestions for improvement in those specific areas. One of them—Chapter Five, on integrating methodologists and substantive experts in research teams—also appeared in *Studies in Intelligence*. Chapter Nine contains several broad recommendations, including suggestions for further research.

To the extent possible, I tried to avoid using professional jargon. Even so, the reader will still find a number of specific technical terms, and, in those cases, I have included their disciplinary definitions as footnotes.

A Work in Progress

In some respects, it may seem strange or unusual to have an anthropologist perform this type of work rather than an industrial/organizational psychologist or some other specialist in professional performance improvement or business processes. The common perception of cultural anthropology is one of fieldwork among indigenous peoples. Much has changed during the past 40 years, however. Today, there are many practitioners and professional associations devoted to the application of anthropology and its field methods to practical problem-solving in modern or postindustrial society.[9]

It is difficult for any modern anthropological study to escape the legacy of Margaret Mead. She looms as large over 20th century anthropology as does Sherman Kent over the intelligence profession. Although Franz Boas is arguably the father of American anthropology and was Margaret Mead's mentor, hers is the name everyone recognizes and connects to ethnography.[10] Chances are, if one has read anthropological texts, one has read Mead.

---

[9] The Society for Applied Anthropology and the National Association for the Practice of Anthropology section of the American Anthropological Association are the two principal anthropological groups. Another group is the Inter-University Seminar on Armed Forces and Society, a professional organization representing 700 social science fellows, including practicing anthropologists, applying their research methods to issues in the military.

I mention Mead not only because my work draws heavily on hers, but also because of her impact on the discipline and its direction. She moved from traditional cultural anthropological fieldwork in the South Pacific to problem-oriented applied anthropology during World War II. She was the founder of the Institute for Intercultural Studies and a major contributor to the Cold War RAND series that attempted to describe the Soviet character. She also pioneered many of the research methods that are used in applied anthropology today. I mention her work also as an illustrative point. After two years of field research in the South Pacific, she wrote at least five books and could possibly have written more.

As I look over the stacks of documentation for this study, it occurs to me that, given the various constraints of the fellowship, there is more material here than I will be able to address in any one text. There are the notes from 489 interviews, direct observations, participant observations, and focus groups; there are personal letters, e-mail exchanges, and archival material; and there are my own notes tracking the progress of the work. Moreover, the fieldwork continues. As I write this, I am scheduling more interviews, more observations, and yet more fieldwork.

This text, then, is more a progress report than a final report in any traditional sense. It reflects findings and recommendations to date and is in no way comprehensive. Finally, based as it is on my own research interests and research opportunities, it is but one piece of a much larger puzzle.

---

[10] Boas (1858–1942) developed the linguistic and cultural components of ethnology. His most notable work was *Race, Language, and Culture* (1940).

PART I

Research Findings

eth•nog•ra•phy\n [**F** *ethnographie*, fr. *ethno-* + *-graphie* -graphy] (1834) : the study and systematic recording of human cultures: *also*: a descriptive work produced from such research. (*Merriam Webster's Collegiate Dictionary, Eleventh Edition*)

CHAPTER ONE
Definitions

Because I conducted human performance–related fieldwork before I came to this project, I carried into it a certain amount of experiential bias, or "cognitive baggage." The research findings from those other studies could bias my perspective and research approach within the Intelligence Community. For example, surgeons and astronauts do not need to deal with intentionally deceptive data. Patients are not trying to "hide" their illnesses from surgeons, and spacecraft are not thinking adversaries intent on denying astronauts critical pieces of information. This one difference may mean that intelligence analysis is much more cognitively challenging than the other two cases and that the requisite psychomotor skills are significantly less important. In an effort to counteract the biases of experience, I will attempt to be explicit about my own definitions in this work.

Working Definitions

The three main definitions used in this work do not necessarily represent definitions derived from the whole of the intelligence literature. Although some of the definitions used in this work are based on the Q-sort survey of the intelligence literature described later, some are based on the 489 interviews, focus groups, and two years of direct and participant observations collected during this project.

Definition 1: Intelligence is secret state or group activity to understand or influence foreign or domestic entities.

The above definition of *intelligence*, as used in this text, is a slightly modified version of the one that appeared in Michael Warner's work in a recent article in *Studies In Intelligence*.[1] Warner reviews and synthesizes a number of previous attempts to define the discipline of intelligence and comes to the conclusion that "*Intelligence is secret state activity to understand or influence foreign entities.*"

Warner's synthesis seems to focus on strategic intelligence, but it is also logically similar to actionable intelligence (both tactical and operational) designed to influence the cognition or behavior of an adversary.[2] This synthesis captures most of the elements of actionable intelligence without being too restrictive or too open-ended, and those I asked to define the word found its elements, in one form or another, to be generally acceptable. The modified version proposed here is based on Warner's definition and the interview and observation data collected among the law enforcement elements of the intelligence agencies. These elements confront adversaries who are not nation states or who may not be foreign entities. With this in mind, I chose to define intelligence somewhat more broadly, to include nonstate actors and domestic intelligence activities performed within the United States.

Definition 2: Intelligence analysis is the application of individual and collective cognitive methods to weigh data and test hypotheses within a secret socio-cultural context.

This meaning of *intelligence analysis* was harder to establish, and readers will find a more comprehensive review in the following chapter on developing an intelligence taxonomy. In short, the literature tends to divide intelligence analysis into "how-to" tools and techniques or cognitive processes. This is not to say that these items are mutually exclusive; many authors see the tools and techniques of analysis as cognitive processes in themselves and are reluctant to place them in different categories. Some authors tend to perceive intelligence analysis as essentially an individual cognitive process or processes.[3]

My work during this study convinced me of the importance of making explicit something that is not well described in the literature, namely, the very

---

[1] Michael Warner, "Wanted: A Definition of 'Intelligence'," *Studies in Intelligence* 46, no. 3 (2002): 15–22.

[2] US Joint Forces Command, *Department of Defense Dictionary of Military and Associated Terms.*

[3] The appendix lists literature devoted to each of these areas.

interactive, dynamic, and social nature of intelligence analysis. The interview participants were not asked to define intelligence analysis as such; rather, they were asked to describe and explain the process they used to perform analysis. The interview data were then triangulated with the direct and participant observation data collected during this study.[4]

Despite the seemingly private and psychological nature of analysis as defined in the literature, what I found was a great deal of informal, yet purposeful collaboration during which individuals began to make sense of raw data by negotiating meaning among the historical record, their peers, and their supervisors. Here, from the interviews, is a typical description of the analytic process:

> *When a request comes in from a consumer to answer some question, the first thing I do is to read up on the analytic line. [I] check the previous publications and the data. Then, I read through the question again and find where there are links to previous products. When I think I have an answer, I get together with my group and ask them what they think. We talk about it for a while and come to some consensus on its meaning and the best way to answer the consumer's question. I write it up, pass it around here, and send it out for review.[5]*

The cognitive element of this basic description, "when I think I have an answer," is a vague impression of the psychological processes that occur during analysis. The elements that are not vague are the historical, organizational, and social elements of analysis. The analyst checks the previous written products that have been given to consumers in the past. That is, the analyst looks for the accepted organizational response before generating analytic hypotheses.

The organizational-historical context is critical to understanding the meaning, context, and process of intelligence analysis. There are real organizational and political consequences associated with changing official analytic findings and releasing them to consumers. The organizational consequences are associated with challenging other domain experts (including peers and supervisors). The potential political consequences arise when consumers begin to question the veracity and consistency of current or previous intelligence reporting. Accurate or not, there is a general impression within the analytic community

---

[4] In research, triangulation refers to the application of a combination of two or more theories, data sources, methods, or investigators to develop a single construct in a study of a single phenomenon.

[5] Intelligence analyst's comment during an ethnographic interview. Such quotes are indented and italicized in this way throughout the text and will not be further identified; quotes attributable to others will be identified as such.

that consumers of intelligence products require a static "final say" on a given topic in order to generate policy. This sort of organizational-historical context, coupled with the impression that consumers must have a final verdict, tends to create and reinforce a risk-averse culture.

Once the organizational context for answering any given question is understood, the analyst begins to consider raw data specific to answering the new question. In so doing, the analyst runs the risk of confirmation biases. That is, instead of generating new hypotheses based solely on raw data and then weighing the evidence to confirm or refute those hypotheses, the analyst begins looking for evidence to confirm the existing hypothesis, which came from previous intelligence products or was inferred during interactions with colleagues. The process is reinforced socially as the analyst discusses a new finding with group members and superiors, often the very people who collaborated in producing the previous intelligence products. Similarly, those who review the product may have been the reviewers who passed on the analyst's previous efforts.

This is not to say that the existing intelligence products are necessarily inaccurate. In fact, they are very often accurate. This is merely meant to point out that risk aversion, organizational-historical context, and socialization are all part of the analytic process. One cannot separate the cognitive aspects of intelligence analysis from its cultural context.

Definition 3: Intelligence errors are factual inaccuracies in analysis resulting from poor or missing data; intelligence failure is systemic organizational surprise resulting from incorrect, missing, discarded, or inadequate hypotheses.

During interviews, participants were asked to explain their understanding of the terms *intelligence error* and *intelligence failure*. There was little consensus regarding the definitions of error and failure within the Intelligence Community or within the larger interview sample. Here are some sample responses:

I don't know what they mean.

There are no such things. There's only policy failure.

You report what you know, and, if you don't know something, then it isn't error or failure. It's just missing information.

Failure is forecasting the wrong thing.

Failure is reporting the wrong thing.

Error is forecasting the wrong thing.

Error is reporting the wrong thing.

A failure is something catastrophic, and an error is just a mistake.

Error is about facts; failure is about surprise.

Error is when nobody notices, and failure is when everybody notices.

Some responses disavowed the existence of intelligence error and failure; some placed the terms in the broader context of policy and decisionmaking; some interchanged the two terms at random; some defined the terms according to their outcomes or consequences. Despite the variability of the responses, two trends emerged: novice analysts tended to worry about being factually inaccurate; senior analysts, managers, and consumers, tended to worry about being surprised. Often, participants' responses were not definitions at all but statements meant to represent familiar historical examples:

The attack on Pearl Harbor.

The Chinese sending combat troops into Korea.

The Tet Offensive.

The Soviet invasion of Afghanistan.

The collapse of the Soviet Union.

The Indian nuclear test.

September Eleventh.

The danger of defining by example is that each case is contextually unique and can be argued ad infinitum. What is important about these examples as a whole is that they all indicate one central and recurring theme. Specifically, all these examples signify surprise—in some cases, intelligence surprise; in other cases, military, civil, and political surprise. Even if the Intelligence Community itself was not surprised by one of these events, it was unable to convince the military, civil, and political consumers of intelligence that these events might occur; in which case, the failure was one of communication and persuasion.

When I began this study, my own definition of error and failure derived from the psychological and cognitive disciplines. Specifically, I took it that human error and failure are related to measures of cognitive and psychomotor accuracy, commission of error being at one end of the accuracy scale and omission or not performing the correct action being at the other.[6]

---

[6] See Appendix A for a list of literature on error.

During the interviews for this study, I soon found that the psychological definition was insufficient. The psychological definition took into account the cognitive and psychomotor components of task-structure, time-to-task, and accuracy-of-task as measures of errors and error rates, but it did not fully take into account the notion of surprise.[7] Surprise is the occurrence of something unexpected or unanticipated. It is not precisely commission or omission; it indicates, rather, the absence of contravening cognitive processes. Measures of accuracy may account for factual errors in the intelligence domain, but measures of accuracy are insufficient to account for surprise events and intelligence failure.

To put this in context, an analyst, while accounting successfully for an adversary's capability, may misjudge that adversary's intention, not because of what is cognitively available, but because of what is cognitively absent. The failure to determine an adversary's intention may simply be the result of missing information or, just as likely, it may be the result of missing hypotheses or mental models about an adversary's potential behavior.

---

[7] Sociological definitions are more akin to the definitions proposed in this study. Failure can occur due to system complexity and missing data as well as through the accumulation of error. See Charles Perrow, *Normal Accidents. Living with High Risk Technologies.* I'd like to thank Dr. Perrow for his assistance with this work.

CHAPTER TWO
Findings

———————◆———————

Scientific knowledge, like language, is intrinsically the common property of a group or else nothing at all. To understand it we shall need to know the special characteristics of the groups that create and use it.

Thomas Kuhn[1]

The more we learn about the world, and the deeper our learning, the more conscious, specific, and articulate will be our knowledge of what we do not know.

Karl Popper[2]

The purpose of this research was to identify and describe conditions and variables that negatively affect intelligence analysis, to develop relevant and testable theory based on these findings, and to identify areas in which strategies to improve performance may be effective. Although there has recently been a great deal of concern that intelligence error and failure rates are inordinately high, in all likelihood, these rates are similar to those of other complex socio-cognitive domains, such as analysis of financial markets. The significant differences are that other complex domains employ systematic performance

---

[1] Philosopher of science Thomas Kuhn described the now-common concept of paradigm shifts in scientific revolutions. He posited that paradigm shifts are tied to cultural and social constructionist models, such as Vygotsky's (See footnote 22 in Chapter Three). Thomas Kuhn, *The Structure of Scientific Revolutions.*
[2] Karl Popper was one of the 20th century's pre-eminent philosophers of science. Karl Popper, *Conjectures and Refutations: The Growth of Scientific Knowledge.*

improvement infrastructures and that the consequences of intelligence error and failure are disproportionately high in comparison with other domains.

It is evident from the literature that intelligence organizations recognize the need to improve their performance and that it is possible to make the domain of intelligence analysis into a coherent scientific discipline. The first step in this transition is to identify and describe performance gaps.[3] Once gaps have been identified, it will be possible to introduce performance improvement methods systematically and to measure the effectiveness of the results. This work is intended to further research toward creating intelligence organizations that are more effective.

The Problem of Bias

Although a researcher might pretend to be neutral and unbiased in presenting his findings and conclusions, personal biases can creep into a finished product. The methods ethnographers employ to collect raw data and the use of interpretational analysis to extract meaning and generate theory virtually guarantee it. In my view, one should be candid about this possibility. I noted in Chapter One that ethnographers bring a certain amount of experiential baggage to their work, myself included. At this point, before discussing analytical difficulties and problems I identified during my research, I want to make the readers aware of an additional personal bias that has developed from observing the Intelligence Community.

During my research, I developed a great deal of empathy for individual analysts and the problems they face in trying to perform their jobs. The reason for this is straightforward and something every anthropologist recognizes. It is part of the process that anthropologists reach a point where they can modify their own identity in order to gain insight into a different culture. The risk is that empathy and identity modification will induce the researcher to "go native" and produce bias in his findings.

Although I may empathize with analysts personally, it is critical for theory development to avoid parroting the views, kudos, or complaints of individual analysts, who may or may not be dissatisfied with their unique professional experience. In order to counteract the empathy bias, I employed multiple data collection techniques and then used those data to refute or confirm each categorical finding. Triangulation is not an infallible system, however, and the reader is advised to approach these findings with both a critical eye and the

---

[3] Performance gaps are the difference or distance between ideal (perfect) organizational performance and organizational performance. In this case, ideal performance includes complete data sets, reportorial accuracy, and the ability to avoid strategic, operational, and tactical surprise.

foreknowledge that this researcher has a number of personal and professional biases.[4]

Finding: Secrecy Versus Efficacy

Secrecy and efficacy conflict. Secrecy interferes with analytic effectiveness by limiting access to information and sources that may be necessary for accurate or predictive analysis. In turn, openness interferes with security by degrading the value of information resources and by revealing specific sources and methods.

Perfect secrecy would ultimately be unproductive, because it would restrict information to one mind or to a very small group of minds. Limiting available resources in this way would produce organizational failure in competition with resources available to a large and diverse group of adversaries. Perfect openness would also lead to organizational failure, because, with full access to all information, there would never be an instance of advantage for any one group over any other group. In addition, perfect openness would result in adversaries being aware they are under observation and could lead them to alter their behavior to deceive the observer if they so desired.[5]

Between these two extremes, there is some notional point where secrecy and openness converge to create an optimal performance tradeoff. My perception is that, within the Intelligence Community, more organizational emphasis is placed on secrecy than on effectiveness. It is important, in my view, that there be a voice in favor of openness to counterbalance the many voices whose sole or primary responsibility is the advocacy and maintenance of

---

[4] Throughout the project, my data collection method consisted of written field notes. Anthropologists traditionally include specific detail from participant input or direct observation. Usually, this is in the form of precise descriptions of the actual behavior of participants and transcripts of their verbal interactions. It is also standard practice in field work to capture these data, and the data from the interviews and focus groups, on audio- or videotape. These practices were not followed in this particular case for two reasons: first, the nature of my work was not to document actual practices and procedures; rather, it was to derive categories of variables and individual variables in order to create a taxonomy, and to use the prototype taxonomy to structure the interactions; second, the nature of intelligence work and the environment in which it occurs, as well as its professional practitioners, require that certain data be restricted.

[5] This has been demonstrated in the psychological literature and is referred to as the Hawthorne Effect. Derived from research that began with an experimental program at Western Electric's Hawthorne Works conducted between 1927 and 1930, the Hawthorne Theory, broadly interpreted, states that the behavior of subjects changes when they are aware of being observed. See Fritz J. Roethlisberger and William J. Dickson, *Management and the worker*; Elton Mayo, *The Human Problems of an Industrial Civilization*.

Secrecy vs. Efficacy

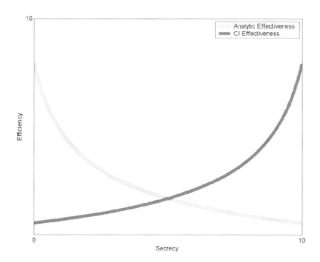

secrecy. I believe this secrecy-efficacy conflict can be stated as a theory, along the following lines.[6]

The more open the system (where zero is perfect information access and sharing on the X axis secrecy scale [as shown on the above graph]), the more access an analyst has to all sources of information within the Intelligence Community regarding an adversary. In addition, this openness encourages interorganizational communication, interaction, and sharing of information among analysts and increases the likelihood that an analyst will be more efficient (in this case the Y axis efficiency scale) and therefore effective or accurate in his or her assessment of a situation.

Conversely, counter-intelligence is negatively affected by zero-level secrecy and perfect openness. The less open or more compartmentalized the system, the more efficient and effective are counterintelligence activities. Notionally, the two curves would meet somewhere in the tradeoff between efficiency and secrecy. Where they meet would depend on program goals and a clear definition of starting points and end-states.

The notional set of curves above illustrates the tradeoff between system efficiency and system secrecy and the effect that the tradeoff has on performance effectiveness, both positive and negative. In this case, the starting and ending points of effectiveness for analysis and for counterintelligence are arbitrary and could be positioned anywhere along a continuum between zero

---

[6] I would like to credit and thank Matthew Johnson at the Institute for Defense Analyses for his help in formulating this theory.

and ten. In this theory, analytic efficiency and effectiveness are purely functions of system openness and do not take into account analytic methods or personnel.

This theory will require additional refinement, and it may or may not be represented by a tradeoff curve like the one proposed here. The theory will also require numerous controlled quantitative experiments to test its explanatory power.

Finding: Time Constraints

The work itself is a 24-hour-a-day job, but it never seems like I have any time to actually analyze anything when I'm at my desk. I spend most of my time reading daily traffic, answering e-mail, coordinating papers with everybody, and writing. Mostly I read and write, but when the workday is over, I go home and think. It isn't like I can turn off my brain. So, I guess I do most of my real analysis on my own time.

The majority of the analysts interviewed indicated that time was one of their greatest constraints at work. This comment triangulated with the findings from direct and participant observation. In addition, analysts indicated that there has been a communitywide shift toward focusing on short-term issues or problem solving, thereby addressing the immediate needs of intelligence consumers. This shift in product focus, coupled with a growth in available all-source raw intelligence, has resulted in a change in the pace of analytic production. In order to generate the daily products, analysts have had to change the way they go about doing their work.

I haven't been doing this very long, but I wish I had been a journalism major instead of poli-sci. The pace is excruciating.

I don't get much sleep. It's like cramming for finals, except we do it every day.

Everything I do is reactive. I don't have time to work my subject. We're not pro-active here.

I'm so busy putting out today's fires, I don't have any time to think about what kind of catastrophe is in store for me a month from now.

About 15 years ago, I used to have 60 percent of my time available for long-term products. Now, it's between 20 and 25 percent.

I probably have about 30 percent of my time for self-initiated products.

You know, someday somebody is bound to notice that velocity isn't a substitute for quality. We've gotten rid of the real analytic products that we use to make, and now we just report on current events.

Not all analysts indicated that time constraints and information load had a negative effect on their performance. A minority indicated that there was sufficient time to perform analytic duties and prepare analytic products.

This is a tactical shop. It's all we do. Current reporting is our job.

I work a slow desk. I have plenty of time for self-initiated products —maybe 60 percent or more.

I multitask pretty well. I don't really experience a time-crunch.

Maybe I just process better than other people, but I don't really feel pressed for time. Besides, I'd rather be at a hot desk than at a cold desk.

Analytic supervisors were more evenly mixed in their opinions about time constraints. A slight majority of the managers interviewed said time constraints had negative effects on the work environment, work processes, and the morale of their staff. A majority of them also put analytic time constraints in a larger context of policy making. They indicated that the decision-cycle of policymakers was 24 hours a day and that their responsibility was to support that decision cycle with current intelligence.

In discussing their perceptions of consumer demand, the managers' views of the nature of those demands were mixed.

I want my analysts to produce long-term products. I want them thinking through their subjects. The decision makers want well-thought-out products, not just daily briefs.

Our customers want current production. They never complain about the daily products and, frankly, I doubt they have time to read the longer stuff.

My consumers like the bigger pieces. They like having the context and broader picture. They don't want to be spoon fed.

I've never had a customer tell me they want more to read.

Our customers want to avoid surprise. As long as we keep them from being surprised, I don't care if we do daily or long-term production. I don't think they care either.

Finding: Focus on Current Production

The present daily production cycle and the focus on current intelligence also affect group interactions and the analytic process.

Group Interactions:

It doesn't matter if I'm writing a piece myself or if I'm coordinating a piece with some group. We don't sit around and test hypotheses, because we're too busy writing. We've got serious deadlines here.

If, by group analysis, you mean the senior expert in the room tells everybody what he thinks, and then we generally agree so that we can get back to our own deadlines, then, sure, there's a group process.

We used to have groups that did current reporting and different groups that did longer term products. We still have some of that, but it is very limited. I couldn't say what happened exactly, but we're all doing current production now.

The Analytic Process:

People seem to have confused writing with analyzing. They figure that if you just go through the mechanics of writing something, then you must have analyzed it. I don't know about everybody else, but it doesn't work that way for me. I need time to think through the problem.

Our products have become so specific, so tactical even, that our thinking has become tactical. We're losing our strategic edge, because we're so focused on today's issues.

Alternative analysis is a nice concept, but I don't have the time to do it. I've got to keep up with the daily traffic.

I use several analytic techniques that are relatively fast. Scenario development, red teams, competing hypotheses, they're all too time consuming.

We've got Bayesian tools, simulations, all kinds of advanced methods, but when am I supposed to do any of that? It takes all my time to keep up with the daily reporting as it is.

I don't have time to worry about formal analytic methods. I've got my own system. It's more intuitive and a lot faster.

Finding: Rewards and Incentives

The shift in the analytic production cycle is not only reflected in the products and processes but also in the way analysts perceive the system by which intelligence organizations reward and promote employees. Employees see their opportunities for promotion as being tied directly to the number of daily products they generate and the amount of social capital or direct consumer influence they amass, most often when their work is recognized by senior policymakers.[7]

> *In any given week, I could devote about 20 percent of my time to longer think pieces, but why should I? You can write all the think pieces you want, but, if you don't write for the daily briefs, you aren't going to move into management. These days the only thing that matters is getting to the customers.*

> *If I write a 12-page self-directed piece that goes out as a community product, and somebody else writes one paragraph with two bullet points that goes into a daily brief, the guy who got in the daily brief is going to get the recognition. Why waste my time with the big products?*

> *It isn't really official policy, but the reality is that sheer production equals promotion. People talk about quality, but, in the end, the only measurable thing is quantity.*

> *Our group has a "team award" of 5,000 bucks. Last year, they gave it to the one guy who published the most. I'm not sure how that one guy won a "team award," but there you go.*

> *Technically, I have four bosses. The only thing that seems to keep them all happy is volume. It's like piece work.*

> *Quality? How do you measure quality? Quantity—now that's something you can count.*

> *Promotion is based on production—pure and simple.*

In sum, aside from specific tactical groups, staff positions that generate limited social capital, and individual cognitive differences, there is a majority sentiment among the analysts interviewed that the combination of a shorter

---

[7] Social capital refers to the set of norms, social networks, and organizations through which people gain access to power, resources, and reciprocity and through which decisionmaking and policy creation occur. In other words, whom you know is just as important as what you know. Pierre Bourdieu, "The Forms of Capital"; Robert Putnam, "The Prosperous Community" and *Bowling Alone*. See also the empirical work on social capital summarized in Tine Feldman and Susan Assaf, *Social Capital: Conceptual Frameworks and Empirical Evidence*.

production cycle, information load, a shift in product focus, and organizational norms regarding promotion have had an impact on analytic work and intelligence analysis itself.

Finding: "Tradecraft" Versus Scientific Methodology

> *Human beings do not live in the objective world alone, nor alone in the world of social activity as ordinarily understood, but are very much at the mercy of the particular language which has become the medium of expression for their society...The fact of the matter is that the "real world" is to a large extent unconsciously built upon the language habits of the group...We see and hear and otherwise experience very largely as we do because the language habits of our community predispose certain choices of interpretation.*

Edward Sapir[8]

The Intelligence Community, in its culture and mythos and in its literature, tends to focus on intelligence *operations* rather than on intelligence *analysis*. Open literature about the community certainly does so. Along with time constraints and the analytic production cycle, the private and public focus on operations has had an effect on intelligence analysts and analytic methodology. The principal effect is the spread of the concept of "tradecraft" within the analytic community.

Community members quite often used the word "tradecraft" to describe intelligence analysis during the interviews, observations, training programs, workshops, and actual analytic tasks that I performed for this study. Analysts, managers, instructors, and academic researchers employed the word "tradecraft" as a catchall for the often-idiosyncratic methods and techniques required to perform analysis. Although the intelligence literature often refers to tradecraft, the works tend to be a collection of suggestions and tips for writing and communicating with co-workers, supervisors, and consumers instead of focusing on a thorough examination of the analytic process and techniques.

The notion that intelligence operations involve tradecraft, which I define as *practiced skill in a trade or art*, may be appropriate, but the analytic community's adoption of the concept to describe analysis and analytic methods is not. The obvious logical flaw with adopting the idea of tradecraft as a standard of practice for analytic methodology is that, ultimately, analysis is neither craft nor art. Analysis, I contend, is part of a *scientific* process. This is an important

---

[8] Edward Sapir is best known for the Sapir-Whorf hypothesis, which asserts linguistic/cognitive relativity (language and thought are inseparable; therefore, different languages mean different ways of thinking). Edward Sapir, *Language*.

distinction, for language is a key variable in anthropology and often reveals a great deal about the cognition and culture of a community of interest.[9]

The adoption by members of the analytic community of an inappropriate term for the processes and methods employed in their professional lives obfuscates and complicates the reality of their work. The adoption of the word "tradecraft" demonstrates the analytic community's need to create a professional identity separate and unique from other disciplines but tied directly to the perceived prestige and cachet of intelligence operations. Adopting "tradecraft" as a term of reference for explaining work practices and as a professional identity marker may seem trivial. Yet the term, and its effect on the community, has unanticipated consequences.

Tradecraft purposefully implies a mysterious process learned only by the initiated and acquired only through the elaborate rituals of professional indoctrination. It also implies that the methods and techniques of analysis are informal, idiosyncratic, unverifiable, and perhaps even unexplainable. "Good" methods are simply those that survive, and then are passed on by "good" analysts to novice analysts. Unfortunately, "good" in both instances is not an objective measure. That is, there is no formal system for measuring and tracking the validity or reliability of analytic methods, because they are both perceived and employed within the context of idiosyncratic tradecraft. When asked to describe the analytic process, analysts responded in a variety of ways.

> *First, I figure out what I know and what I don't know about some situation. Then, I look for information to fill the gap.*

> *I have a model of the situation in my head. Whenever something new comes in, I see if it fits with the model. If it does, I add it to the model; if it doesn't, I try to figure out why.*

> *I've found a system that lets me keep up. I just look for anomalies. When I see any novel data, then I worry.*

> *I'm always looking for anything strange or out of place. Then, I source it to see if it is meaningful.*

> *The current data ought to fit a certain pattern. If it doesn't, I know something is wrong.*

> *First, I print the daily traffic I'm concerned with; then I lay out all of the relevant stuff in front of me on my desk or the floor; then I start looking for threads.*

---

[9] The literature on this subject is extensive. For a representative list, see the appendix.

I'm looking for links and patterns. Once I figure out the pattern, I can figure out where to look next.

I use patterns. If things start happening, out of the ordinary things, I pay attention to them.

I try to build patterns out of the data. It helps me predict what will happen next.

I come up with a few scenarios and see what the evidence supports.

I look for data that are diagnostic: some piece of evidence that rules out certain possibilities.

I try to weigh the evidence to see which scenario it supports.

Although anomaly-detection, pattern-recognition, and weighing data may appear to be idiosyncratic tradecraft based on individual expertise and cognitive skills, these methods can be formalized and replicated if the operating parameters, variables, and rules of evidence are made explicit.[10] This is to say that intelligence analysis can be reconstructed in the context of a scientific method, which is merely an articulated, formal process by which scientists, collectively and over time, endeavor to put together a reliable, consistent, and nonarbitrary representation of some phenomena. Broadly, the steps include:

- observation and description of phenomena;

- formulation of hypotheses to explain phenomena;

- testing of hypotheses by independent experts;

- refutation or confirmation of hypotheses.

These steps do not suggest that any specific scientific methodology results in what is ultimately the truth, rather that scientific methods are merely formal processes used to describe phenomena, make predictions, and determine which hypothesis best explains those phenomena. The principal value of any type of methodological formalism is that it allows other researchers to test the validity and reliability of the findings of any other researcher by making explicit, and therefore replicable, the means by which anyone reaches a specific conclusion.[11]

The idea that intelligence analysis is a collection of scientific methods encounters some resistance in the Intelligence Community. The interview data analyzed in this study highlight many subtle—and not so subtle—prejudices

---

[10] A corollary to these methods can be found in the practice of radiologists. See Chapter Five for more on expertise.

that analysis is not a science. That is, it is an art or craft in which one can attain skill but not a formal discipline with tested and validated methodology.

What we do is more art and experience than anything else.

Science is too formal. We can't actually run experiments here.

How would you actually test a hypothesis in intelligence?

Science is what you do in a lab.

We're not scientists; we're analysts. We don't generate the data.

We don't worry too much about theory; we worry about the facts.

In my discipline, I might be a scientist, but, in intelligence, I am a practitioner.

I use science for my area, but I don't think intelligence analysis is science.

As long as intelligence analysis continues to be tradecraft, it will remain a mystery. The quality of any tradecraft depends on the innate cognitive capabilities of the individual and the good fortune one has in finding a mentor who has discovered, through many years of trial and error, unique methods that seem to be effective. This process of trial and error is, in general, similar to any scientific process, except that the lessons learned in tradecraft, unlike those of other disciplines, often occur without being captured, tested, or validated.

In an oral tradition, individual tradecraft methods are passed on by means of apprenticeship. The consequence for any culture tied to an oral tradition is the loss of important knowledge that occurs with the loss of practitioners. In organizations, the retirement of experts and innovators leads to the loss of that expertise and innovation, unless there is some formal written and educational system to keep that knowledge alive. [12]

The data collected through both interviews and observation indicated that there were, in fact, general methods that could be formalized and that this process would then lead to the development of intelligence analysis as a scientific discipline. The principal difficulty lies not in developing the methods them-

---

[11] Rather than engage in the longstanding and ongoing debate in the academic community about what is and what is not science or a scientific method, suffice it to say that any scientific method needs to be explicit, replicable, and refutable. The literature surrounding this debate is voluminous. The philosophy of science, logic, language, and epistemology has taken this debate in a number of directions. There is, however, a general theme that replication is a key ingredient to any scientific method.

[12] See section on Endangered Languages in Barbara Grimes, ed., *Ethnologue*. 14th ed.

selves, but in articulating those methods for the purpose of testing and validating them and then testing their effectiveness throughout the community. In the long view, developing the science of intelligence analysis is easy; what is difficult is changing the perception of the analytic practitioners and managers and, in turn, modifying the culture of tradecraft.

Finding: Confirmation Bias, Norms, and Taboos

Organization is key, because it sets up relationships among people through allocation and control of resources and rewards. It draws on tactical power to monopolize or parcel out liens and claims, to channel action into certain pathways while interdicting the flow of action into others. Some things become possible and likely; others are rendered unlikely.

Eric Wolf[13]

Time constraints affect both the general analytic production cycle and analytic methodology by contributing to and exacerbating cognitive biases. Although there are any number of cognitive biases to which the human mind is susceptible, one in particular became evident during the triangulation phase and interpretive analysis of the interview and observation data of this study. The cognitive bias identified most often was confirmation bias, which is the tendency of individuals to select evidence that supports rather than refutes a given hypothesis.[14]

Although the psychological mechanism by which confirmation bias occurs is in debate, confirmatory behavior is a consistent finding throughout the experimental psychology and cognitive science literature. Rather than focus on the mechanism and nomenclature, the term "confirmation bias" is used in this work as a description of confirmatory behavior. This behavior was

---

[13] Eric Wolf was an anthropologist who focused on power, social structures, and the third world. His work on power and the lives of peasants is considered a modern anthropological classic. Eric Wolf, *Pathways of Power.*

[14] There is a fair amount of disagreement in the psychological literature regarding the mechanism by which an individual displays confirmatory behavior. Some researchers attribute it to motivational factors, for example, a desire to maintain respect within a group. Other researchers attribute it to selectivity factors, an unconscious cognitive selection of data that confirms the current status quo. Some researchers attribute it to social factors, a subspecies of groupthink (see Irving Janis, *Groupthink*). Still others ascribe it to a misapplication of heuristics, whereby an individual learns a set of rules that solves one problem and then begins using that same set of rules to try to solve other types of problems. Although the literature is extensive, Karl Popper's *The Logic of Scientific Discovery* provides a foundation for understanding the issue. Jonathan Evans' *Bias in Human Reasoning: Causes and Consequences* is still a useful and concise summary of the research related to confirmation bias.

described by participants during the interviews and observed during direct and participant observations throughout the fieldwork.

Analysts were asked to describe the work processes they employed to answer questions, solve problems, describe and explain phenomena, make forecasts, and develop intelligence products. The process they described began with an examination of previous analytic products developed by their organization in order to establish a baseline from which they could build their own analysis.

> *When a request comes in from a consumer to answer some question, the first thing I do is to read up on the analytic line.*

> *The first thing I do is check the pervious publications, and then I sort through the current traffic.*

> *I've looked at our previous products, and I've got a good idea of the pattern; so, when I sort through the traffic, I know what I'm trying to find.*

> *I try to keep up with all the products that come out of our area, so I know where to start my piece.*

A literature search is often the first step in any research endeavor. The utility of this practice is not merely to define and understand the current state of research in the field but also to determine major controversies and divergences of opinion. Trying to discern controversies and divergence in intelligence products is often difficult, because some of them—national intelligence estimates (NIE), in particular—are specifically designed to produce a corporate consensus for an audience of high-level policymakers.

These products can and do include divergent opinions, in the form of footnotes, but these tend to indicate inter-, rather than intra-, organizational differences. Dissenting footnotes are products of the coordination process, the result of an inability on the part of one or several community organizations to convince the others of a particular point of view. Not surprisingly, the least probable opinion is often the hardest to defend, whereas the most probable opinion is the easiest to support.

The literature search approach may promote a logical consistency among analytic products, but it has the unintended consequence of imposing on the analyst using it a preexisting mental model of the phenomena in question. The existing analytic products describe, implicitly or explicitly, a set of working hypotheses that an analyst may wish to reflect in his or her own work. Of course, these existing hypotheses are rarely tested each time they are incorporated into new products. What tends to occur is that the analyst looks for current data that confirms the existing organizational opinion or the opinion that seems most probable and, consequently, is easiest to support. As this strategy is also the most time-efficient technique, it reduces the time constraints associated with the daily production cycle.

This tendency to search for confirmatory data is not necessarily a conscious choice; rather, it is the result of accepting an existing set of hypotheses, developing a mental model based on previous corporate products, and then trying to augment that model with current data in order to support the existing hypotheses. Although motivational and heuristic factors and a tendency toward "groupthink" might contribute to confirmatory behavior in intelligence analysis, my observations and interviews during this study suggest that the predominant influence is selectivity bias in order to maintain a corporate judgment.

The maintenance of a corporate judgment is a pervasive and often-unstated norm in the Intelligence Community, and the taboo against changing the corporate product line contributes to confirmation biases. Once any intelligence agency has given its official opinion to policymakers, there exists a taboo about reversing or significantly changing the official or corporate position to avoid the loss of status, trust, or respect. Often, policymakers perceive a change in judgment as though the original opinion was wrong, and, although unstated, there are significant internal and external social pressures and consequences associated with being perceived as incorrect.

An analyst can change an opinion based on new information or by revisiting old information with a new hypothesis; in so doing, however, he or she perceives a loss of trust and respect among those with whom the original judgment was shared. Along with this perceived loss of trust, the analyst senses a loss of social capital, or power, within his or her group.[15]

It is even more difficult for an intelligence agency to change its official position once it has made its judgments known to those outside of the organization. There is a sense that changing the official product line will be seen outside of its context—the acquisition of new information, for instance—and that it will be perceived by the policymakers as an example of incompetence or, at least, of poor performance on the part of the intelligence agency.

This perception then carries with it the threat of a loss in status, funding, and access to policymakers, all of which would have a detrimental effect on the ability of the intelligence agency to perform its functions. In short, it serves the interest of the intelligence agency to be perceived as decisive

---

[15] Reciprocity in this case has to do with information, judgment, and trust. The classic anthropological text on social reciprocity and trust within and between groups is Marcel Mauss's *The Gift*. Originally published in 1950 and based in part on the work of his uncle and mentor, Emile Durkheim, Mauss's work (*Essai sur le Don* in its French version) lays the foundation for his contention that reciprocity is the key to understanding the modern concept of social capital.

instead of academic and contradictory, and that message is transmitted to the analysts. In response to the organizational norm, the analyst is inclined to work the product line rather than change it.

> *Our products are company products, not individual products. When you publish something here, it's the official voice. It's important for us to speak with one voice.*

> *It doesn't do us any good if people think we can't make up our mind.*

> *Access matters; if people think you don't know what you're talking about, then they stop seeing you.*

> *We already briefed one thing. I can't go in there and change it now. We'll look like idiots.*

> *When I was new, I wrote a piece that disagreed with our line. Let's just say, I'm more careful about that now.*

Another organizational norm that contributes to confirmation bias in the Intelligence Community is the selection and weighing of data according to classification. Secrets carry the imprimatur of the organization and, in turn, have more face validity than information collected through open sources.[16]

Most analysts indicated that they considered "secret" data collected by covert means to be more important or meaningful than "open" or unclassified data. Analysts said that they rely on open sources to help fill in missing pieces of their mental models but that they test the model's validity with secret information. Choosing to rely on classified data as more meaningful to problem solving and as a tool for testing the validity of their hypotheses serves to exacerbate the confirmation bias.

> *I'm an all-source analyst, so I use whatever I can get my hands on; but, if the traffic comes from operations, I tend to pay more attention to it than to information in the open literature.*

> *There is something special about the word "secret" in my business. It says that it must be important because people had to go and get it rather than its just showing up in the news. We tend to weigh classified material as more important than other sources.*

---

[16] In research methodology, face validity is the concept that a measurement instrument *appears* or *seems* to measure what it is actually intended to measure and requires no theoretical supporting material. In contrast, content validity depends on the content of the domain and established theories to determine its measures of validity. See David Brinberg and Joseph McGrath, *Validity and the Research Process*; Edward Carmines and Richard Zeller, *Reliability and Validity Assessment*; Jerome Kirk and Marc Miller, *Reliability and Validity in Qualitative Research*; Mark Litwin, "How to measure survey reliability and validity"; William Trochim, *The Research Methods Knowledge Base*.

> *We get all kinds of sourced material, but I think I trust technical col-
> lection more than the other INTs.*

> *I try to use everything we get, but, if we are jammed, I rely on
> sources we collect.*

> *Our value-added is classified sourcing. Everybody has access to the
> Web and CNN.*

> *All our customers are analysts these days. What we bring to the
> party is information no one else has.*

> *We're in the business of secrets. If you see that stamped on some-
> thing, it must be there for a reason.*

The over reliance on classified information for hypothesis testing creates a situation in which the data are screened and sorted by the organization before they are selected and tested by the analysts. Classified information comes from very specific types of technical and human sources, and it is filtered through very specific reporting channels. It also has a tendency to become homogeneous because of the source types and reporting mechanisms. Because it is generated and packaged in specific formats using specific processes, classified information lacks the diversity that is inherent in open information, and this contributes to confirmation bias.

In sum, operating under difficult time constraints, trying to make new work accord with previous products, trying to maintain the prestige and power of the organization, and assigning greater weight to secret information than to open information have a cumulative effect, and the analyst often finds himself or herself trying to produce daily products using the most time-efficient strategies available instead of generating or testing hypotheses by way of refutation.

The persistence of the notion of tradecraft, coupled with organizational norms, promotes the use of disjointed analytic strategies by separating intelligence analysts from other scientific disciplines. These conditions have had an effect on the self-concept of analysts and have molded the way analysts perceive their own identity.

Finding: Analytic Identity

> *The self is something which has a development; it is not initially
> there, at birth, but arises in the process of social experience and
> activity, that is, develops in the given individual as a result of his
> relations to that process as a whole and to other individuals within
> that process.*

> George Mead.[17]

Asked to define their profession, the majority of analysts described the process of analysis rather than the actual profession. The question, "What is an intelligence analyst?" resulted most often in a description of the work day and of the production cycle of analytic products and very seldom in an explanation of analytic methodology or a definition of an analyst outside of some specific context. With very few exceptions, analysts did not describe intelligence analysis as its own discipline with its own identity, epistemology, and research tradition.

This is not necessarily uncommon. When physicians are asked to describe their profession, they tend to respond with a specific subdiscipline: "I'm a cardio-thoracic surgeon," for example. When asked for a more general description, however, they tend to respond, "I'm a doctor" or "I'm a physician." That is, in selective, insular professional cultures, practitioners are able to define their role in both a specific and general fashion. Intelligence analysts had difficulty defining their professional identity in a general way and often relied on specific context to explain what it is that they do and, by extension, who they are.

The perception of individual analysts regarding their professional identity was associated most often with their organization's function or with their own educational background and not with intelligence analysis as its own unique discipline.

I work counternarcotics.

I work counterterrorism.

I'm a military analyst.

I'm a leadership analyst.

I'm an economist.

I'm a political scientist.

In addition to these categories, many analysts described their professional identity in terms of intelligence collection methods or categories.

I do all-source analysis.

I'm a SIGINT analyst.

I'm an IMINT analyst.

I'm a technical analyst.

---

[17] George Mead was an American pragmatist philosopher and social psychologist, who, with John Dewey, made the University of Chicago the home of pragmatist philosophy and the "Chicago School" of sociology at the end of the 19th century. George Mead, *Mind, Self, and Society.*

The shift in focus to daily analytic products, the changes in the production cycle, and a heterogeneously defined professional discipline have had an additional effect on the professional identity of analysts within the Intelligence Community. Analysts often commented that they perceived their job and their daily work routine as more akin to reporting than to analysis.

> *Basically, on a day-to-day basis, it's like working at CNN, only we're CNN with secrets. Actually, it's more like CNN's* Headline News.

> *Imagine* USA Today *with spies—bullet points, short paragraphs, the occasional picture. You know, short and simple.*

> *I think of myself as a writer for the most important newspaper in the world.*

Many analysts expressed dissatisfaction with the shift in work processes from long-term forecasts and toward current reporting and the subsequent shift in their own professional identity within the Intelligence Community. The current sentiment about identity was often contrasted against an idealized past that was described as being freer of current production practices and products.

> *About 15 years ago, I would have described myself as a scholar. Now, I'm a reporter. I've got 15 people trying to change my work into bullet points. Presumably, nobody has time to read anymore.*

> *When I joined, it seemed that the word "analyst" was shorthand for "problem solver." Now, it's shorthand for "reporter."*

> *I'm proud of where I work. I'm proud of the job that we do. But, it is hard to take pride in one paragraph. I have to look at the big picture, or I would get discouraged.*

> *I spend most of my waking hours doing this, but I still can't really say what an analyst is.*

> *I'm not a reporter, and I'm not an academic. I'm somewhere in between.*

The heterogeneous descriptions and definitions of intelligence analysis as a professional discipline were consistent findings during this study, indicating that there needs to be a clear articulation and dissemination of the identity and epistemology of intelligence analysis. A clearly defined professional identity would help to promote group cohesion, establish interagency ties and relationships, and reduce intra- and interagency communication barriers by establishing a professional class throughout the Intelligence Community. At an individual level, a clearly defined professional identity helps to reduce job dissatisfaction and anxiety by giving larger meaning to an individual's daily actions.[18]

Finding: Analytic Training

When I started, there wasn't much training available. There were a few advanced courses, but, for the most part, it was on the job.

A professional identity is generally a disciplinary norm, and it regularly occurs in other domains that are as cognitively demanding as intelligence analysis, such as medicine, aeronautics, and jurisprudence. These other domains practice a general system of professional enculturation that progresses from a basic education program to specialized training.[19] These training programs help to differentiate communities of practitioners from the general public, create specific and unique professional identities, and develop basic communication and task-specific skills. They also help the profession to continue to advance through formal research efforts.

This is not the case within the Intelligence Community as a whole. Generally, the intelligence agencies that do provide basic and advanced training do so independently of other intelligence organizations.[20] A number of intelligence agencies do not provide basic analytic training at all or have only recently begun to do so, relying instead on on-the-job experiences and informal mentoring.

We haven't had a culture of training analysts here in the past. It's only in the last year or so that we've started to change that.

When I started here, analysts were considered administrative personnel. We didn't have a training program. I think they just started one this year.

My background was technical analysis, and we had a lot of operational training where I used to work. But now that I'm doing more strategic analysis, I've had to make it up as I go along.

---

[18] Philip Cushman, *Constructing the Self, Constructing America*; Anthony Giddens, *Modernity and Self-Identity*; John P. Hewitt, *Self and Society*; Lewis P. Hinchman and Sandra K. Hinchman, *Memory, Identity, Community*; Carl Jung, *The Undiscovered Self*; George Levine, ed., *Constructions of the Self*.

[19] Enculturation is the process or mechanism by which a culture is instilled in a human being from birth until death. In this instance, professional enculturation refers to the acquisition of a professional identity through specific cultural rituals and practices, as displayed, for example, by practitioners who have graduated from medical school, law school, and basic military training.

[20] See footnote 7 in the Introduction for several recent cross-agency training initiatives.

We have a basic training program, but it is different from the other agencies. Our mission is different. The problem is that we talk past each other all the time.

When I got hired, I had an advanced degree. People assumed that, if I had a Masters, I could just figure out what I was supposed to do.

The focus of training within the community varies widely and is shaped by the mission of the agency, such as technical, tactical, and operational. Many spend a considerable amount of time teaching new analysts how to prepare briefings, write papers, and perform administrative functions unique to their agency. This is logical from the perspective of agency managers, who naturally believe that investments made in personnel, training, and readiness ought to be tailored specifically for their own organizations.

The problem with an agency-centric view is that, without a general communitywide training program for intelligence analysts, agencies and their analysts have difficulty finding, communicating, and interacting with one another.[21] Analysts often said they were disinclined to draw on resources outside of their own agency, indicating that either they do not know whom to contact or their experience in the past has been influenced by a strict organizational focus.

The media keep talking about intelligence failures and communication breakdowns in the Intelligence Community. What do they expect? We don't even speak the same language.

It's taken me 15 years to build my own network. If I didn't have my own contacts, I wouldn't know who to call.

I don't bother going outside. Our focus is different here.

We have official channels, but it only really works if you trust the person on the other end of the phone. That's hard to do if you don't know them.

Without an inclusive communitywide basic training program, differentiation between the intelligence analysis discipline, as a whole, and other fields of study is unlikely. A community of practitioners will have difficulty interacting with one another, communicating between and within organizations, and establishing a professional identity, which is a key ingredient in the development of a professional discipline.

---

[21] Stephen Marrin, *CIA's Kent School: A Step in the Right Direction* and "Improving CIA Analysis by Overcoming Institutional Obstacles."

PART II

Ethnography of Analysis

Taxonomy of Intelligence Analysis Variables

Systemic Variables	Systematic Variables	Idiosyncratic Variables	Communicative Variables
Organization	User Requirements	Weltanschauung	Formal
Internal	Operations	(worldview)	Inter-organization
Structure	Information Acquisition	Affiliation	Hierarchical
Leadership	Collection Methods	Familial	Inter-division
Culture	Overt	Cultural	Inter-group
History	Covert	Ethnic	Intra-organization
Traditions	Information Reliability	Religious	Hierarchical
Social Practice	Reproducible	Social	Intra-division
Taboo	Consistent	Linguistic	Intra-group
Group Characteristics	Information Validity	Political	Individual
Hierarchy	Historical	Psychology	Hierarchical
Resources & Incentives	Single Source	Bias	Inter-division
Manpower	Dual Source	Personality Profile	Intra-group
Budget	Triangulation	Security Trust	Informal
Technology	Information Archive	Cognitive Processing	Inter-organization
Assets	Storage	Learning Style	Hierarchical
R&D	Access	Information Acquisition	Inter-division
Facilities	Correlation	Information Processing	Inter-group
Work Groups-Teams	Retrieval	Expertise	Intra-organization
External	Analytical Methodology	Problem-solving	Hierarchical
Consumer Needs	Approach	Decisionmaking	Intra-division
Time and Imperatives	Intuitive	Cognitive Load	Intra-group
Consumer Use	Structured	Speed/Accuracy	Individual
Consumer Structure	Semi-structured	Stress Effects	Hierarchical
Consumer Hierarchy	Information Processing	Education	Inter-group
Conumer Reporting	Historical Information	Domain	Intra-group
Politics	Current Information	Location	Technology
Internal-Organization	Decision Strategies	Mentor	Networked Analysis
Policy	Estimative	Training	Collaboration
Tradition	Predictive	Organizational	
Taboo	Reporting	Domain	
Security/Access	Verbal Methods	Procedural	
External-National	Written Methods	Readiness	
Law		Resources	
Policy		Facilities	
External-International			
Security			
Denial			
Deception			
Policy			

CHAPTER THREE

A *Taxonomy of Intelligence Variables*[1]

———◆———

Science is organized knowledge.

Herbert Spencer[2]

Aristotle may be the father of scientific classification, but it was biologist Carolus Linnaeus who introduced the first formal taxonomy—kingdom, class, order, genera, and species—in his *Systema Naturae* in 1735. By codifying the naming conventions in biology, Linnaeus's work provided a reference point for future discoveries. Darwin's development of an evolutionary theory, for example, benefited greatly from Linnaeus's creation of a hierarchical grouping of related organisms. The *Systema Naturae* taxonomy was not a fixed product but rather a living document. Linnaeus himself revised it through 10 editions, and later biologists have continued to modify it.[3]

In response to new discoveries and the development of new research methods in other domains, taxonomies were created to help organize those disciplines and to assist researchers in identifying variables that required additional study. The development of specific taxonomies—from highly structured systems, such as the periodic table of chemical elements, to less structured approaches, such as Bloom's Taxonomy[4]—is a key step in organizing knowl-

---

[1] A version of this chapter, "Developing a Taxonomy of Intelligence Analysis Variables," originally appeared in *Studies in Intelligence* 47, no. 3 (2003): 61–71.

[2] Herbert Spencer's *The Study of Sociology*, published in 1874, set the stage for the emergence of sociology as a discipline.

[3] Ernst Haeckel introduced *phylum* to include related classes and *family* to include related genera in 1866. The Linnaeus taxonomy is currently being revised to accommodate genomic mapping data.

edge and furthering the growth of individual disciplines. A taxonomy differentiates domains by specifying the scope of inquiry, codifying naming conventions, identifying areas of interest, helping to set research priorities, and often leading to new theories. Taxonomies are signposts, indicating what is known and what has yet to be discovered.

This chapter, to which more than 100 individuals contributed their time and advice, proposes a taxonomy for the field of intelligence. It is my hope that the resulting organized listing of variables will help practitioners strengthen their understanding of the analytic process and point them in directions that need additional attention.

Intelligence Analysis

> *We could have talked about the science of intelligence, but . . . the science of intelligence is yet to be invented.*

Charles Allen[5]

Developing an intelligence taxonomy is complicated by the fact that the literature in the field is episodic and reflects specialized areas of concern. Perhaps it is best to begin with what appears to be a key distinction between general analysis and intelligence analysis, that of solving a problem in the public domain, and solving a problem in a private or secret domain.

Ronald Garst articulates two arguments that are used to support this distinction: intelligence analysis is more time sensitive than analysis in other domains and it deals with information that intentionally may be deceptive.[6] The notion that intelligence is uniquely time sensitive is questionable, however. Intelligence is not the only domain where time constraints can force decisions to be made before data are complete. Time is always a key variable, whether one is in an operating room or in a cockpit. To be sure, intelligence is a life and death profession, but so are medicine and mass transportation. In each instance, failure can mean casualties.

Garst's point about intentional deception is more germane. With the possible exception of business and financial markets, analysts in other fields seldom deal with intentional deception. As discussed in Chapter One, Michael Warner makes a good case for secrecy being the primary variable distinguish-

---

[4] See Benjamin S. Bloom, *Taxonomy of Educational Objectives*. Bloom's taxonomy is a classification of levels of intellectual behavior in learning, including knowledge, comprehension, application, analysis, synthesis, and evaluation.

[5] Comment made by the Associate Director of Central Intelligence for Collection at a public seminar on intelligence at Harvard University, spring 2000.

[6] Ronald Garst, *A Handbook of Intelligence Analysis*.

ing intelligence from other such activities.[7] He argues that the behavior of the subject of intelligence changes if the subject is aware of being observed or analyzed. As discussed earlier, Warner's argument is supported by a long history of psychological research, beginning with an experimental program between 1927 and 1930 at Western Electric's Hawthorne Works in Chicago.[8]

Intentional deception can occur outside intelligence—in connection with certain law enforcement functions, for example—but most of the professional literature treats this as the exception rather than the rule. In the case of intelligence analysis, deception *is* the rule; the validity of the data is always in doubt. Moreover, intelligence analysts are specifically trained to take deception into account as part of the analytic process—to look for anomalies and outliers instead of focusing on the central tendencies of distribution.

The taxonomy being developed here requires a definition of intelligence analysis that is specific to the field. Intelligence pioneer Sherman Kent, who saw intelligence as a "special category of knowledge," laid the foundation for understanding the activities inherent in intelligence analysis by demonstrating that the analytic process itself was subject to being analyzed.[9] Kent's approach to analysis was to reduce the process to smaller functional components for individual study.[10] For example, he described intelligence analysis as having a basic descriptive element, a current reporting element, and an estimative element.

Following suit, other authors focused attention on the process or methodological elements of intelligence analysis. In *Intelligence Research Methodology*, Jerome Clauser and Sandra Weir followed Kent's three functional areas and went on to describe basic research foundations and the inductive and deductive models for performing intelligence analysis.[11] Garst's *Handbook of Intelligence Analysis* contains less background in basic research methods than Clauser and Weir's book, but it is more focused on the intelligence cycle.[12]

Bruce Berkowitz and Allan Goodman highlight the process of strategic intelligence and define intelligence analysis as: "[T]he process of evaluating and transforming raw data into descriptions, explanations, and conclusions for intelligence consumers."[13] Lisa Krizan, too, focuses on process. She writes

---

[7] Michael Warner.

[8] The Hawthorne Effect. See footnote 5 in Chapter Two.

[9] Sherman Kent, *Strategic Intelligence for American World Policy*.

[10] See Chapter Seven for a fuller discussion of this approach, now usually referred to as meta-analysis.

[11] Jerome K. Clauser and Sandra M. Weir, *Intelligence Research Methodology*.

[12] See also: Morgan Jones, *The Thinker's Toolkit*. Jones's book is a popular version of the work of Garst and Clauser and Weir in that it describes a collection of analytic methods and techniques for problem-solving; however, the methods are not necessarily specific to intelligence.

that, "At the very least, analysis should fully describe the phenomenon under study, accounting for as many relevant variables as possible. At the next higher level of analysis, a thorough explanation of the phenomenon is obtained, through interpretation of the significance and effects of its elements on the whole."[14] In addition, several authors have written about individual analytic approaches.[15]

Although the referenced works focus on methods and techniques, they do not suggest that analysis is limited to these devices. The view that analysis is both a process and a collection of specific techniques is explicit in the above definitions. Analysis is seen as an action that incorporates a variety of tools to solve a problem. Different analytic methods have something to offer different analytic tasks.

Although largely implicit in the above definitions, analysis is also seen as a product of cognition, and some authors directly link the two. Robert Mathams defines analysis as: "[T]he breaking down of a large problem into a number of smaller problems and performing mental operations on the data in order to arrive at a conclusion or generalization."[16] Avi Shlaim writes: "Since the facts do not speak for themselves but need to be interpreted, it is inevitable that the individual human propensities of an intelligence officer will enter into the process of evaluation."[17] Yet others describe analysis as a process whereby: "[I]nformation is compared and collated with other data, and conclusions that also incorporate the memory and judgment of the intelligence analyst are derived from it."[18]

Several authors make the case that analysis is not just a product of cognition but is itself a cognitive process. J. R. Thompson and colleagues write that "[I]ntelligence analysis is an internal, concept-driven activity rather than an external data-driven activity."[19] In his *Psychology of Intelligence Analysis*, Heuer observes: "Intelligence analysis is fundamentally a mental process, but understanding this process is hindered by the lack of conscious awareness of the workings of our own minds."[20] Ephraim Kam comments: "The process of intelligence analysis and assessment is a very personal one. There is no agreed-upon analytical schema, and the analyst must primarily use his belief

[13] Bruce D. Berkowitz and Allan E. Goodman, *Strategic Intelligence for American National Security*, 85. See Chapter Four for more on the intelligence cycle.

[14] Lisa Krizan, *Intelligence Essentials for Everyone*.

[15] See the apprendix for a listing of the literature.

[16] Robert Mathams, "The Intelligence Analyst's Notebook."

[17] Avi Shlaim, "Failures in National Intelligence Estimates: The Case of the Yom Kippur War."

[18] John Quirk et al., *The Central Intelligence Agency: A Photographic History.*

[19] J. R. Thompson, R. Hopf-Weichel, and R. Geiselman, *The Cognitive Bases of Intelligence Analysis.*

[20] Richards J. Heuer, Jr., *Psychology of Intelligence Analysis.*

system to make assumptions and interpret information. His assumptions are usually implicit rather than explicit and may not be apparent even to him."[21]

These definitions reflect the other end of the spectrum from those concerned with tools and techniques. They suggest that the analytic process is a construction of the human mind and is significantly different from individual to individual or group to group. Certainly, Kam goes farthest along this path, but even he does not suggest that one forgo tools; rather, he says that the process of choosing the tool is governed by cognition as well.

Recognizing that the scope of intelligence analysis is so broad that it includes not only methods but also the cognitive process is a significant step. Viewing analysis as a cognitive process opens the door to a complex array of variables. The psychology of the individual analyst must be considered, along with individual analytic tools. In the broadest sense, this means not merely understanding the individual psyche but also understanding the variables that interact with that psyche. In other words, *intelligence analysis is the socio-cognitive process,*[22] *occurring within a secret domain, by which a collection of methods is used to reduce a complex issue to a set of simpler issues.*

Developing the Taxonomy

> *The first step of science is to know one thing from another. This knowledge consists in their specific distinctions; but in order that it may be fixed and permanent distinct names must be given to different things, and those names must be recorded and remembered.*
>
> Carolus Linnaeus

My research was designed to isolate variables that affect the analytic process. The resulting taxonomy is meant to establish parameters and to stimulate dialogue in order to develop refinements. Although a hierarchic list is artificial and rigid, it is a first step in clarifying areas for future research. The actual variables are considerably more fluid and interconnected than such a structure suggests. Once the individual elements are refined through challenges in the literature, they might be better represented by a link or web diagram.[23]

To create this intelligence analysis taxonomy, I used Alexander Ervin's applied anthropological approach, which employs multiple data collection methods to triangulate results.[24] I also drew on Robert White's mental work-

---

[21] Ephraim Kam, *Surprise Attack: The Victim's Perspective*, 120

[22] That is, analysis does not occur in a vacuum. It is socially constructed. See Lev Vygotsky, *Mind and Society.*

[23] See Chapter Four for Judith Meister Johnston's systems analysis approach to describing the fluidity of the intelligence process.

load model, David Meister's behavioral model, and the cognitive process model of Gary Klein and his colleagues.[25] Each model focuses on a different aspect of human performance: White's examines the actual task and task requirements; Meister's looks at the behavior of individuals performing a task; and Klein's uses verbal protocols to identify the cognitive processes of individuals performing a task.

Surveying the literature. My research began with a review of the literature, both for background information and for the identification of variables. The intelligence literature produced by academics and practitioners tends to be episodic, or case-based. This is not unique to the field of intelligence. A number of disciplines—medicine, business, and law, for example—are also case-based. Many of the texts were general or theoretical rather than episodic. Again, this is not an uncommon phenomenon. The review yielded 2,432 case studies, journal articles, technical reports, transcripts of public speeches, and books related to the topic. I then narrowed the list to 374 pertinent texts on which a taxonomy of intelligence analysis could be built, and I analyzed them to identify individual variables and categories of variables that affect intelligence analysis.[26]

Using a methodology known as "Q-Sort," by which variables are sorted and categorized according to type, I read each text and recorded the variables that each author identified.[27] These variables were then sorted by similarity into groups. Four broad categories of analytic variables emerged from this process.[28]

Refining the prototype. Next, I used the preliminary taxonomy derived from my reading of the literature to structure interviews with 51 substantive experts and 39 intelligence novices. In tandem, I conducted two focus group sessions, with five individuals in each group. As a result of the interviews and focus group discussions, I added some variables to each category, moved some to different categories, and removed some that appeared redundant.

Testing in a controlled setting. Finally, to compare the taxonomy with specific analytic behaviors, I watched participants in a controlled intelligence analysis–training environment. Trainees were given information on specific

---

[24] Alexander Ervin, *Applied Anthropology.* See Chapter One, note 4 for a definition of triangulation.

[25] Robert White, *Task Analysis Methods*; David Meister, *Behavioral Analysis and Measurement Methods*; G. Klein, R. Calderwood, and A. Clinton-Cirocco, *Rapid Decision Making on the Fire Ground.*

[26] A copy of the list and search criteria is available from the author.

[27] William Stephenson, *The Study of Behavior: Q-Technique and its Methodology.* See Chapter Eleven for additional information on this methodology.

[28] I would like to credit Dr. Forrest Frank of the Institute for Defense Analyses for his suggestions regarding the naming convention for the categories of variables in the accompanying chart.

cases and directed to use various methods to analyze the situations and to generate final products. During the training exercises, the verbal and physical behavior of individuals and groups were observed and compared with the taxonomic model. I participated in a number of the exercises myself to gain a better perspective. This process corroborated most of the recommendations that had been made by the experts and novices and also yielded additional variables for two of the categories.

The resulting taxonomy is purely descriptive. It is not intended to demonstrate the weight or importance of each variable or category. That is, the listing is not sufficient to predict the effect of any one variable on human performance. The intention of the enumeration is to provide a framework for aggregating existing data and to create a foundation for future experimentation. Once the variables have been identified and previous findings have been aggregated, it is reasonable to consider experimental methods that would isolate and control individual variables and, in time, indicate sources of error and potential remediation

Systemic Variables

The column of Systemic Variables incorporates items that affect both an intelligence organization and the analytic environment. Organizational variables encompass the structure of the intelligence organization; leadership, management, and management practices; history and traditions; the working culture, social practices within the organization, and work taboos; and organizational demographics. They also include internal politics, the hierarchical reporting structure, and material and human resources. Industrial and organizational psychology, sociology, and management studies in business have brought attention to the importance of organizational behavior and its effect on individual work habits and practices. The works of Allison, Berkowitz and Goodman, Elkins, Ford, Godson, and Richelson, among others, examine in general the organizational aspects of intelligence.[29]

Systemic Variables

Organization
  Internal
    Structure
    Leadership
    Culture
      History
        Traditions
      Social Practice
        Taboo
      Group Characteristics
    Hierarchy
    Resources and Incentives
      Manpower
      Budget
      Technology
      Assets
      R&D
      Facilities
    Work Groups-Teams
  External
    Consumer Needs
    Time and Imperatives
    Consumer Use
    Consumer Structure
    Consumer Hierarchy
    Conumer Reporting
Politics
  Internal-Organization
    Policy
    Tradition
    Taboo
    Security/Access
  External-National
    Law
    Policy
  External-International
    Security
      Denial
      Deception
    Policy

Systematic Variables
User Requirements
Operations
Information Acquisition
Collection Methods
Overt
Covert
Information Reliability
Reproducible
Consistent
Information Validity
Historical
Single Source
Dual Source
Triangulation
Information Archive
Storage
Access
Correlation
Retrieval
Analytical Methodology
Approach
Intuitive
Structured
Semi-structured
Information Processing
Historical Information
Current Information
Decision Strategies
Estimative
Predictive
Reporting
Verbal Methods
Written Methods

The Systemic Variables category also focuses on environmental variables. These include such external influences on the organization as consumer needs and requirements, time limitations, and methods for using the information; and the consumer's organization, political constraints, and security issues. The works of Betts, Hulnick, Hunt, Kam, and Laqueur address the environmental and consumer issues that affect intelligence analysis.[30] Case studies that touch on various systemic variables include: Allison, on the Cuban missile crisis; Betts, on surprise attacks; Kirkpatrick, on World War II tactical intelligence operations; Shiels, on government failures; Wirtz, on the Tet offensive in Vietnam; and Wohlstetter, on Pearl Harbor.[31]

Systematic Variables

The Systematic Variables are those that affect the process of analysis itself. They include the user's specific requirements, how the information was acquired, the information's reliability and validity, how the information is stored, the prescribed methods for analyzing and processing the information, specific strategies for making decisions about the information, and the methods used to report the information to consumers.

A number of authors have written about the analytic tools and techniques used in intelligence, among them Clauser and Weir, on intelligence research methods; Jones, on analytic techniques; and Heuer, on alternative competing hypotheses.

---

[29] Graham T. Allison, *Essence of Decision*; Bruce D. Berkowitz and Allan E. Goodman, *Best Truth*; Dan Elkins, *An Intelligence Resource Manager's Guide*; Harold Ford, *Estimative Intelligence*; Roy Godson, *Comparing Foreign Intelligence*; Jeffrey Richelson, *The U.S. Intelligence Community*.

[30] Richard K. Betts, "Policy-makers and Intelligence Analysts: Love, Hate or Indifference"; Arthur S. Hulnick, "The Intelligence Producer-Policy Consumer Linkage: A Theoretical Approach"; David Hunt, Com*plexity and Planning in the 21st Century*; Kam, *Surprise Attack;* Walter A. Laqueur, *The Uses and Limits of Intelligence*.

[31] Allison; Richard K. Betts, *Surprise Attack*; Lyman B. Kirkpatrick, Jr., *Captains Without Eyes: Intelligence Failures in World War II*; Frederick L. Shiels, P*reventable Disasters: Why Governments Fail*; James J. Wirtz, *The Tet Offensive: Intelligence Failure in War*; Roberta Wohlstetter, *Pearl Harbor: Warning and Decision.*

Comparatively little work has been done comparing structured techniques to intuition. Robert Folker's work is one of the exceptions; it compares the effectiveness of a modified form of alternative competing hypotheses with intuition in a controlled experimental design. His study is unique in the field and demonstrates that experimental methods are possible. Geraldine Krotow's research, on the other hand, looks at differing forms of cognitive feedback during the analytic process and makes recommendations to improve intelligence decisionmaking.[32]

Idiosyncratic Variables

Variables in the third column are those that influence individuals and their analytic performance. These include the sum of life experiences and enculturation—familial, cultural, ethnic, religious, linguistic, and political affiliations—that identify an individual as a member of a group. I have used the German word *Weltanschauung* (customarily rendered in English as "world view") to denote this concept. These idiosyncratic variables also encompass such psychological factors as biases, personality profiles, cognitive styles and processing, cognitive loads,[33] expertise, approach to problem-solving, decisionmaking style, and reaction to stress. Finally, there are such domain variables as education, training, and the readiness to apply knowledge, skills, and abilities to the task at hand.

Idiosyncratic Variables
Weltanschauung (world-view)
Affiliation
Familial
Cultural
Ethnic
Religious
Social
Linguistic
Political
Psychology
Bias
Personality Profile
Security Trust
Cognitive Processing
Learning Style
Information Acquisition
Information Processing
Expertise
Problem-solving
Decisionmaking
Cognitive Load
Speed/Accuracy
Stress Effects
Education
Domain
Location
Mentor
Training
Organizational
Domain
Procedural
Readiness
Resources
Facilities

The relevant psychological literature is extensive. Amos Tversky and Daniel Kahneman began to examine psychological biases in the early 1970s.[34] Their work has found its way into the intelligence literature through Butterfield,

---

[32] Geraldine Krotow, *The Impact of Cognitive Feedback on the Performance of Intelligence Analysts*, 176.

[33] "Cognitive loads" are the amount/number of cognitive tasks weighed against available cognitive processing power.

[34] Amos Tversky and Daniel Kahneman, "The Belief in the 'Law of Small Numbers'" and "Judgment Under Uncertainty: Heuristics and Biases."

Davis, Goldgeier, and Heuer, among others.[35] Decisionmaking and problem-solving have been studied since the early 1920s, and these topics are reflected in Heuer's work as well.[36] Personality-profiling, too, is well understood and has had an impact on recent intelligence practices and theory.[37]

Other well-researched areas, however, have yet to be studied in the context of intelligence. Acculturation and enculturation, educational factors, and training strategies, for example, may yet yield interesting results and insights into the field of intelligence.[38]

Communicative Variables

The fourth category contains variables that affect interaction within and among groups. Because communication is the vital link within the system—among processes and among individuals—this group of variables logically could be included in each of the other three categories. Its broad relevance, however, makes it seem reasonable to isolate it as a distinct area of variability. The Communicative Variables include formal and informal communications within an organization (from products to e-mails), among organizations, and between individuals and the social networks they create. In his essay on estimative probability, Kent highlights this area by describing the difficulty that producers of intelligence have in communicating the likelihood of an event to their consumers.[39] In addition to addressing organizational issues, case studies by Wohlstetter and others touch on communication and social networks and the impact that communication

Communicative Variables
Formal
Inter-organization
Hierarchical
Inter-division
Inter-group
Intra-organization
Hierarchical
Intra-division
Intra-group
Individual
Hierarchical
Inter-division
Intra-group
Informal
Inter-organization
Hierarchical
Inter-division
Inter-group
Intra-organization
Hierarchical
Intra-division
Intra-group
Individual
Hierarchical
Inter-group
Intra-group
Technology
Networked Analysis
Collaboration

---

[35] Alexander Butterfield, *The Accuracy of Intelligence Assessment*; Jack Davis, "Combating Mindset"; James M. Goldgeier, "Psychology and Security"; Heuer.

[36] Frank H. Knight, *Risk, Uncertainty and Profit.*

[37] Caroline Ziemke, Philippe Loustaunau, and Amy Alrich, *Strategic Personality and the Effectiveness of Nuclear Deterrence.*

[38] Acculturation is the cultural change that occurs in response to extended firsthand contact between two or more previously autonomous groups. It can result in cultural changes in groups as well as individuals.

[39] Sherman Kent, "Words of Estimative Probability."

has on the analytic process.[40] This is an area that could benefit from additional study.

Conclusion

There is rarely any doubt that the unconscious reasons for practicing a custom or sharing a belief are remote from the reasons given to justify them.

—Claude Levi-Strauss[41]

As it is now practiced, intelligence analysis is art, tradecraft, and science. There are specific tools and techniques to help perform the tasks, but, in the end, it is left to individuals to use their best judgment in making decisions. This is not to say that science is not a part of intelligence analysis. Science is born of organized knowledge, and organizing knowledge requires effort and time. The work on this taxonomy is intended to help that process by sparking discussion, identifying areas where research exists and ought to be incorporated into the organizational knowledge of intelligence, and identifying areas where not enough research has been performed.

There are a number of parallels in the field of medicine, which, like intelligence, is art, tradecraft, and science. To solve problems, practitioners are trusted to use their best judgment by drawing on their expertise. What is important to remember is that there are numerous basic sciences driving medical practice. Biology, chemistry, physics, and all of the subspecialties blend together to create the medical sciences, the foundation on which modern medicine rests. The practice of medicine has been revolutionized by the sciences that underpin its workings.

Intelligence analysis has not experienced that revolution. Unlike medicine, the basic sciences that underpin intelligence are the human sciences, which are considerably more multivariate and more difficult to control. Because of these factors, it is a more complex task to measure "progress" in the human sciences. Even so, there are numerous domains from which intelligence may borrow. Organizational behavior is better understood today than ever before. Problem-solving and decisionmaking have been researched since the 1920s.

---

[40] Wohlstetter.

[41] Claude Levi-Strauss wrote *Structural Anthropology* in 1958, setting the stage for structuralism to emerge as an analytic interpretive method. Broadly, structuralism seeks to explore the inter-relationships (the "structures") through which meaning is produced within a culture. This meaning, according to structural theory, is produced and reproduced through various practices, phenomena, and activities that serve as systems of "signification." A structuralist studies activities as diverse as food preparation and serving rituals, religious rites, games, literary and non-literary texts, and forms of entertainment to discover the ways in which cultural significance develops.

Structural anthropology addresses many of the enculturation and identity issues that affect individual behavior. Cognitive scientists are building models that can be tested in experimental conditions and used for developing new tools and techniques. Sociology and social theory have much to offer in studying social networks and communication.

The organization of knowledge in intelligence is not a small task, but I believe that the effort should be undertaken for the betterment of the profession. The taxonomy proposed here could serve as a springboard for a number of innovative projects, for example: development of a research matrix that identifies what is known and how that information may be of use in intelligence analysis, setting a research agenda in areas of intelligence that have been insufficiently studied, application of research from other domains to develop additional training and education programs for analysts, creation of a database of lessons learned and best practices to build a foundation for an electronic performance support system, integration of those findings into new analytic tools and techniques, and development of a networked architecture for collaborative problem-solving and forecasting. It is my hope that this taxonomy will help intelligence practitioners take steps in some of these new directions.

CHAPTER FOUR

Testing the Intelligence Cycle Through Systems Modeling and Simulation

Judith Meister Johnston[1]
Rob Johnston

Throughout the Intelligence Community, the process of analysis is represented conventionally by a model known as the Intelligence Cycle (See next page). Unfortunately, the model omits elements and fails to capture the process accurately, which makes understanding the challenges and responsibilities of intelligence analysis much more difficult. It also complicates the tasks of recognizing where errors can occur and determining methods for change based on accurate predictions of behavior. Our analysis of the Intelligence Cycle, employing a systems approach and a simulation created to represent it, demonstrated these shortcomings.[2] Because of its wide acceptance and use in training and in discussions of the analytic process, the traditional representation of the Intelligence Cycle will be closely considered in this chapter, especially with regard to its impact on analytic products, its effectiveness, and its vulnerability to error and failure.

The Traditional Intelligence Cycle

The Intelligence Cycle is customarily illustrated as a repeating process consisting of five steps.[3] ***Planning and direction*** encompasses the management of

---

[1] Dr. Judith Meister Johnston is an educational psychologist with expertise in human performance technology and instructional systems design. A Booz Allen Hamilton Associate, she supports human factors work for the Intelligence Community.

[2] Simulation involves the development of a computer-based model that represents the internal processes of an event or situation and estimates the results of proposed actions.

the entire effort and involves, in particular, determining collection requirements based on customer requests. ***Collection*** refers to the gathering of raw data to meet the collection requirements. These data can be derived from any number and type of open and secret sources. ***Processing*** refers to the conversion of raw data into a format analysts can use. ***Analysis and production*** describes the process of evaluating data for reliability, validity, and relevance; integrating and analyzing it; and converting the product of this effort into a meaningful whole, which includes assessments of events and implications of the information collected. Finally, the product is ***disseminated*** to its intended audience.[4]

The Traditional Intelligence Cycle

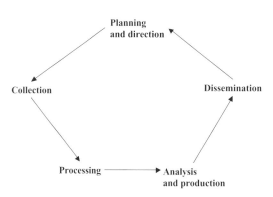

In some ways, this process resembles many other production cycles. It is prescriptive, structured, made up of discrete steps, and expected to yield a specific product. The traditional depiction of the process in the Intelligence Cycle, however, is not an accurate representation of the way intelligence is produced. The notion of a cycle assumes that the steps will proceed in the prescribed order and that the process will repeat itself continuously with reliable results. This type of representation gives the impression that all inputs are constant and flow automatically, but it does not address elements that may influence the movement of the cycle, positively or negatively.

The most significant assumption about the Intelligence Cycle model, that it provides a means for helping managers and analysts deliver a reliable product, should be examined at the outset. This can be accomplished through two types of analyses. The first is a systematic examination of the elements of the process, the inputs it relies on, and the outcomes that can be expected. The second uses a systemic approach to identifying the relationships of the elements in the process and their influence on each other.

---

[3] Central Intelligence Agency, *A Consumer's Guide to Intelligence*.

[4] Central Intelligence Agency, *Factbook on Intelligence*.

Systematic Analysis

Many disciplines (for example, business process, organizational management, human performance technology, program evaluation, systems engineering, and instructional systems design) employ specific methods to analyze the effectiveness of products, programs, or policy implementation. Although they are often given different, domain-specific names and may involve varying levels of detail, these analytic methods involve the identification of *inputs*, *processes*, and *outputs*. Once these elements are identified, the evaluation process maps the relationships of the inputs, their implementation in processes, and their impact on intended—as opposed to actual—outputs.[5] The reasoning underlying this approach is that an effective product, result, or action is one that matches its objectives and that these objectives are reached by processes that logically lead from the objectives to results. Along the way, existing practices and barriers to reaching goals effectively can be identified. Finally, interventions, which can range in complexity from simple job aids to a complete restructuring of the process, can be proposed and implemented and their impacts assessed.[6]

This method of analysis has been employed successfully to evaluate processes that have characteristics similar to the Intelligence Cycle, and we use it here to examine the effectiveness of the Intelligence Cycle and its utility in representing the creation of sound analytic products while avoiding failure or error.

Findings Based on Systematic Analysis

The Intelligence Cycle is represented visually to provide an easy-to-grasp and easy-to-remember representation of a complex process. Although this type of representation may make the flow of information and the interrelationships of steps easy to identify, it does not indicate who or what may affect the completion of a step or the resources needed to begin the next step. In its concise form, then, the visual representation of the Intelligence Cycle is reduced to a map of information handling. Without explicit descriptions of the steps in the process or the benefit of prior knowledge, it can raise questions of accuracy and completeness and can occasion misconceptions, particularly concerning the roles and responsibilities of intelligence analysts.

---

[5] Marc J. Rosenberg, "Performance technology: Working the system."
[6] Roger Kaufman, "A Holistic Planning Model: A Systems Approach for Improving Organizational Effectiveness and Impact."

Inputs, Processes, and Outputs of the Intelligence Cycle

Inputs	Processes	Outputs
Policymaker and other stakeholder questions, requirements	*Direction*	Data collection requirements
Data collection requirements, assessment of available resources and capabilities	*Planning*	Task assignment, potential data sources, focus of analysis
Open-source data: foreign broadcasts, newspapers, periodicals, books; Classified data: case officer, diplomatic, and attaché reports, electronics, satellite photos	*Collection*	Potentially relevant data
Potentially relevant data	*Processing*: Reduction of data in a variety of formats to consistent pieces of usable data	Usable Data
Usable data	*Analysis*: Integration, evaluation, assessment of reliability, validity, and relevance of data	Findings
Analytic review	*Production*: Peer review, supervisory review	Written briefs, studies, long range assessments, short range assessments, oral briefs, national intelligence estimates
Written briefs, studies, long-range assessments, short-range assessments, oral briefs, national intelligence estimates	**Dissemination**	Appropriate product to address customer's need

The table above depicts a more detailed input, process, and output analysis and makes some relationships clearer—for example, the steps that include two actions (planning and direction, analysis and production) have been separated into distinct processes—but it sill leaves a number of questions unanswered. It is difficult to see from this analysis specifically who is responsible for providing inputs, carrying out the processes, and producing outputs; and what requirements are expected of the inputs and outputs.

An important issue that this analysis only partly clarifies is the role of analysts. Nor does it demonstrate how great a burden the process places on them, an especially important point. Assuming that the actions identified in the "Processes" column are ultimately the responsibility of the intelligence analyst, the steps of the process move from a heavy reliance on information coming in from sources outside the analyst's control to a heavy reliance on the analyst to produce and manage the final submission of the product.

Another important defect in this analysis is that steps in the cycle do not accurately represent the differences in the cognitive complexity involved in preparing a long-range assessment or a national intelligence estimate and that required for a two-paragraph brief on a current situation. The same can be said about the process required to develop each of the products.

The Intelligence Cycle depicts a sequential process and does not provide for iterations between steps. This is not an accurate reflection of what happens, particularly in the collection and production steps, where the challenges of defining policymaker needs and shaping collection necessitate repeated refinement of requirements by policymakers or of inferences by the Intelligence Community.

Treverton's "Real" Intelligence Cycle

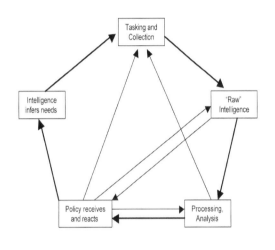

A more accurate picture of the steps in the process and their iterative tendencies may be seen in Greg Treverton's model, which he terms the "Real" Intelligence Cycle (above).[7]

Mark Lowenthal proposes another model.[8] Although presented in a more linear fashion than Treverton's, it focuses on the areas where revisions and reconsiderations take place, representing iteration in a slightly different light. Both models provide a more realistic view of the entire process. In addition, assuming that the analyst's role is represented by the "Processing, Analysis" box, the Treverton model allows us to focus visually and conceptually on the demands that the process can place on the analyst. However, neither model

---

[7] Gregory F. Treverton, *Reshaping National Intelligence in an Age of Information.*
[8] Mark W. Lowenthal, *Intelligence: From Secrets to Policy.*

provides an effective way of showing who is responsible for what, and neither reflects the impact of the work on the individuals responsible for producing the reports—particularly the analyst—nor the reliance of the analyst on a variety of factors beyond his or her control.

In sum, this brief evaluation of the Intelligence Cycle with respect to its inputs, processes, and outputs shows us that the traditional model:

- assumes the process works the same way for all objectives, regardless of complexity and cognitive demands;
- does not represent the iterative nature of the process required for meeting objectives;
- does not identify responsibilities for completing steps and allows for misconceptions in this regard;
- does not accurately represent the impact of resource availability on analysts.

To better understand these limitations and the relationships among elements in the process, it is necessary to step back and take a longer view of the process, using a different method of analysis.

Systemic Analysis

If we think of the phenomenon that is being described by the Intelligence Cycle as a system and perform a systems analysis, we may be able to derive a greater understanding of process relationships, a better representation of the variables affecting the process, and a greater level of detail regarding the process itself.

The premise that underlies systems analysis as a basis for understanding phenomena is that the whole is greater than the sum of its parts. A systems analysis allows for the inclusion of a variety of influences and for the identification of outliers that are obfuscated in other types of analyses but that often play major roles. A systems analysis is accomplished through the examination of phenomena as cause-and-effect patterns of behavior. This approach is called a "closed feedback loop" in systems analysis. It requires a close examination of relationships and their influences, provides a longer view of these relationships, and often reveals new insights based on trends rather than on discrete events.[9]

The systems model diagrammed below is a visual representation of the process. The elements of the Intelligence Cycle are identified in terms of their

---

[9] Fritjof Capra, "Criteria of Systems Thinking"; David L. Kaufman, Jr., *Introduction to Systems Thinking*.

relationships with each other, the flow of the process, and phenomena that influence the elements and the flow. The model uses four icons to represent actions and relationships within the system: stocks, flows, converters, and connectors. The icons and their placement within the systems model show the relationships of the elements of the analyzed phenomenon.

The Components of the Systems Model

Icon	Purpose
Stock	***Stocks*** represent accumulations. These are quantities that can increase or decrease, such as the amount of work that needs to be completed, the time available in which to do it, experience one might bring to a task.
Flow	***Flows*** represent activities. They control the filling or draining of stocks, causing conditions to change.
Converter	***Converters*** change inputs into outputs. They usually represent the variables that initiate change. In the example, a converter might represent a sudden and drastic world event.
Stock Flow Converter	***Connectors*** link elements to other elements, representing assumptions about what depends on what.

The systems model of the Intelligence Cycle provides insights into the process of analysis as well as other factors that can influence the successful and timely completion of an intelligence task. It also provides a way to understand the impact of change in any area of the Intelligence Cycle on other elements, either through reflection or by applying mathematical values to the influences and relationships and running simulations of the model.

Demand. As in the traditional Intelligence Cycle model, the systems model begins with requirements for information that generally come from policymakers. These requirements are represented by a *stock* (found in the upper left-hand quarter of the diagram) because they can increase or decrease based on the level of need for information (a *flow*). The change in level of need is influenced by national and world events, as well as by new questions or requests for clarification of items in previously delivered products. Each request does not contribute equally to the amount of work, which is influenced by the types of documents or products requested, the complexity of the prod-

Systems Model of the Intelligence Cycle

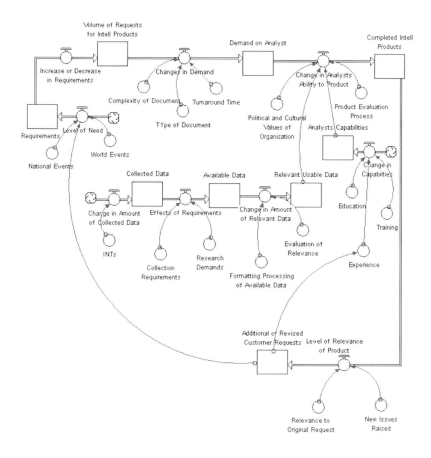

ucts, and the turnaround time imposed. All of these factors determine the level of demand placed on the analyst.

Production. This section focuses on the process of producing intelligence products. The elements described are tied, directly or indirectly, to the flow that represents changes in the analyst's ability to produce. In turn, these changes cause products to be completed and requests of policymakers to be fulfilled. It is important to note that this portion of the model deals with factors that influence the *act* of analysis and does not attempt to address *methods* of analysis.

Factors that influence the ability of analysts to produce are numerous and complex, as shown. First and foremost are the capabilities an analyst brings to the task. This is represented by a *stock*—usually an increasing one—that derives from an analyst's education, training, and experience.

Another influence is the number and frequency of evaluations and revisions imposed on a work in progress. That a draft of the product must be reviewed and edited by a number of others places variable constraints on the time available for creating the original draft. This factor increases in significance when the product requested has a short deadline.

Political and cultural values of the organization also have an influence, usually constraining. Strictly following traditional heuristics and methods and meeting organizational or management expectations may influence both an analyst's ability to produce and the quality of the output. The weight of these influences will vary depending on the experience of the analyst.

Another factor that influences the analyst's ability to produce is the amount of relevant, usable data (a *stock*) available. The term "relevant, usable data" describes all collected intelligence that is relevant to meeting the request and that exists in a format that can be used to develop the product. To become usable, the data must go through steps that are influenced by a variety of *other* people, organizations, systems, and technologies. This process is represented by the stock and flow chain that appears across the middle of diagram.

Data are collected from a variety of sources, represented by the INTs converter.[10] These data add to the stock of collected data. The ways in which accumulated collected data are converted to the stock of available data are influenced by internal research demands and specific collection requirements imposed by analysts, policymakers, and others. Once the data are processed and put into an agreed format for use by intelligence producers and consum-

---

[10] INT is an abbreviation for intelligence, usually contained in acronyms for the various types of intelligence collected by the Intelligence Community, for example, HUMINT (human intelligence) and SIGINT (signals intelligence).

ers, they add to the accumulation of material that affects the ability of an analysts to produce.

Product Influences. The accumulation of completed intelligence products, which is represented as a *stock*, is not in practice an end-state for analysis. A customer may respond to a delivered product by levying additional or revised tasking. In all instances, this information influences the level of need for policymaker requirements and causes the process to begin again. Each iteration of the process is different, not because the steps in the process change, but because those responsible for carrying out the steps have changed as a result of their participation in the previous run. These changes can include a greater level of experience with the process, with the customer, with the topic area, or with the quirks of the organization and its processes. The changes are a manifestation of the concept that the system is greater than the sum of its parts.

Findings Based on Systems Analysis

Systems analysis clearly demonstrates the defects of the traditional Intelligence Cycle model. To recapitulate briefly, the traditional model merely represents a simple list of steps rather than a dynamic closed feedback loop. In addition, although the steps are meant to be performed by several different actors, the model does not provide useful information about what each actually contributes to the cycle, nor does it accurately represent the path a request takes as it is addressed. Another problem with the traditional model is that none of its features help identify ways of developing a consistent product. For example, there is no allowance for a statement of objectives or for any formative or summative evaluations to check that objectives have been met.

On the other hand, the model that resulted from a systems analysis provides a more complex view. That model shows cause and effect, and it shows what other elements have an impact on the development of intelligence products and how and why elements depend on other elements. These advantages of the systems model are clearly apparent in considering the role of analysts in production, a crucial element of the cycle that the traditional model all but ignores.

Impact on Production and Analyst's Control. Study of the systems model shows that the "Analyst's Ability to Produce" (upper right-hand quarter of the diagram) is the central factor in the production cycle and the driver of the feedback loop. The systems view also makes us aware of a less obvious fact that is critically important to a discussion of analytic failure.

A look at the entire system makes readily apparent the number of factors of varying complexity that influence an analyst's ability to produce: the analyst's capabilities; the product evaluation process; the political and cultural values of the organization; the amount of relevant, usable data and actions related to transforming collected data to relevant, usable data; and the level of demand on the analyst. Of these five factors, only one—the analyst's capabilities—is an internal factor and somewhat under the analyst's control.[11] Yet, even though the other factors are out of the analyst's control, the analyst must rely on them to accomplish the goal and to meet the expectations of customers and the organization. When the proportion of external factors to internal factors is as unbalanced as the systems model of the Intelligence Cycle demonstrates, the causes of stress in the analytic environment increase, as does the possibility that stress will occur.

In such a high stress environment, where the critical person is responsible for delivering a product whose development relies on a great number of factors beyond his or her control, there is greater risk of error, with an increased likelihood of incomplete or incorrect products. Tendencies to use shortcuts, to avoid creative thinking, and to minimize the perceived impact of certain events or actions become more apparent in this situation, especially if their implementation means reducing the workload and the stressors. Results of working in such an environment can include increased personnel turnover, missed or undervalued information, lack of attention to detail, decreased motivation, and a lack of creativity in approaching analysis. Moreover, with analysts so central to the process, their actions may have a widespread and, thus, powerful influence on the entire system. This change can be positive or negative. Given the number of elements influencing the analyst that are out of his or her control, however, it is unlikely that the changes would positively affect the quality, accuracy, and number of intelligence products created.

Recommendations

Revisit the traditional intelligence model. The traditional Intelligence Cycle model should either be redesigned to depict accurately the intended goal, or care should be taken to discuss explicitly its limitations whenever it is used. Teaching with an inaccurate aid merely leads to misconceptions that can result in poor performance, confusion, and a need for unlearning and reteaching. If the objective is to capture the entire intelligence process, from the request for a product to its delivery, including the roles and responsibilities of Intelligence Community members, then something more is required. This should be a model that pays particular attention to representing accurately all the elements of the process and the factors that influence them.

---

[11] Even the factors that contribute to the analyst's capabilities, notably experience and training, may be seen to be under the control of others when access to, and selection of, them are considered.

Further Study. The use of simulation allows us to determine flaws in the system that basic informational models cannot address. A simulation moves the image of the Intelligence Cycle from a picture that selectively and indiscriminately illustrates a series of events to a holistic and realistic representation of events, responsibilities, processes, and their impact on each other. The simulation of the Intelligence Cycle developed for this analysis is merely a first step. Further work should be done with it to validate the representations, test for vulnerabilities, predict outcomes, and accurately recommend changes.

Lightening the Analyst's Load. The systems model reveals a serious imbalance in the work processes analysts can and cannot control. It is unrealistic and unnecessary to consider reorganizing the process to correct this defect. However, there are actions that could be taken to provide analysts more control over external factors without significantly altering their roles. These actions would also reduce the amount of potential influence that one group could have over the entire process.

First, analysts might be designated as reports or research analysts. The former would prepare products that address short-term tasks, such as writing for the PDB. As the process of collection and analysis is different for short- and long-term products, this might be a responsibility assigned primarily to more junior analysts. Research analysts might be those with more experience. Freed from the obligation to prepare short-term reports, senior analysts would be available for more intense research efforts, such as those required for an NIE. In addition, cross-training or experience in creating both products and the flexibility to switch from one process to another would provide greater depth of personnel. If appropriate, movement to a long-term research position could be viewed as professional development.

Second, personnel responsible for formatting and processing raw data might be included on accounts. Through association with a particular group, people in this role would have a reasonable idea of analysts' requirements. This would allow the preselection and preparation of data, so that analysts could focus on "connecting the dots." The skills requirement for this role would be akin to those of a research librarian.

Third, tools to help the analyst identify, manage, and fuse relevant data could be identified and deployed. These tools, which need not be limited to those that are technology-based, should be used to support analysts' labor-intensive tasks, thereby freeing them to focus on the analysis of data.

Employ alternative methods for examining work processes. Just as we used alternative methods to examine the Iintelligence Cycle, and as managers press analysts to use alternative analyses in assessing their targets, so should managers employ alternative methods for examining work processes. These methods should not simply test effectivenss; they should also identify vulnerabilities and potential sources of other problems in the community's analytical methods.

PART III

Potential Areas for Improvement

CHAPTER FIVE

Integrating Methodologists into Teams of Experts [1]

Intelligence analysis, like other complex tasks, demands considerable expertise. It requires individuals who can recognize patterns in large data sets, solve complex problems, and make predictions about future behavior or events. To perform these tasks successfully, analysts must dedicate years to researching specific topics, processes, and geographic regions.

Paradoxically, it is the specificity of expertise that makes expert forecasts unreliable. While experts outperform novices and machines in pattern recognition and problem solving, expert predictions of future behavior or events are seldom as accurate as Bayesian probabilities. [2] This is due, in part, to cognitive biases and processing-time constraints and, in part, to the nature of expertise itself and the process by which one becomes an expert.

Becoming an Expert

Expertise is commitment coupled with creativity. By this, I mean the commitment of time, energy, and resources to a relatively narrow field of study and the creative energy necessary to generate new knowledge in that field. It takes a great deal of time and regular exposure to a large number of cases to become an expert.

---

[1] A version of this chapter originally appeared as "Integrating Methodologists into Teams of Substantive Experts in *Studies in Intelligence* 47, no. 1 (2003): 57–65.

[2] Method for estimating the probability of a given outcome developed by Thomas Bayes (1702–61), an English mathematician. See Thomas Bayes, "An Essay Toward Solving a Problem In the Doctrine of Chances."

Entering a field of study as a novice, an individual needs to learn the heuristics and constraints—that is, the guiding principles and rules—of a given task in order to perform that task. Concurrently, the novice needs to be exposed to specific cases that test the reliability of such heuristics. Generally, novices find mentors to guide them through the process of acquiring new knowledge. A fairly simple example would be someone learning to play chess. The novice chess player seeks a mentor who can explain the object of the game, the number of spaces, the names of the pieces, the function of each piece, how each piece is moved, and the necessary conditions for winning or losing a game.

In time, and with much practice, the novice begins to recognize patterns of behavior within cases and, thus, becomes a journeyman. With more practice and exposure to increasingly complex cases, the journeyman finds patterns not only within but also among cases and, more important, learns that these patterns often repeat themselves. Throughout, the journeyman still maintains regular contact with a mentor to solve specific problems and to learn more complex strategies. Returning to the example of the chess player, the individual begins to learn patterns of opening moves, offensive and defensive strategies, and patterns of victory and defeat.

The next stage begins when a journeyman makes and tests hypotheses about future behavior based on past experiences. Once he creatively generates knowledge, rather than simply matching patterns, he becomes an expert. At this point, he becomes responsible for his own knowledge and no longer needs a mentor. In the chess example, once a journeyman begins competing against experts, makes predictions based on patterns, and tests those predictions against actual behavior, he is generating new knowledge and a deeper understanding of the game. He is creating his own cases rather than relying on the cases of others.

The chess example in the preceding paragraphs is a concise description of an apprenticeship model. Apprenticeship may seem to many a restrictive, old-fashioned mode of education, but it remains a standard method of training for many complex tasks. In fact, academic doctoral programs are based on an apprenticeship model, as are such fields as law, music, engineering, and medicine. Graduate students enter fields of study, find mentors, and begin the long process of becoming independent experts and generating new knowledge in their respective domains.

To some, playing chess may appear rather trivial when compared, for example, with making medical diagnoses, but both are highly complex tasks. Chess heuristics are well-defined, whereas medical diagnoses seem more open ended and variable. In both instances, however, there are tens of thousands of potential patterns. A research study discovered that chess masters had spent between 10,000 and 20,000 hours, or more than 10 years, studying and playing chess. On average, a chess master acquires 50,000 different chess patterns.[3]

Similarly, a diagnostic radiologist spends eight years in full-time medical training - four years of medical school and four years of residency—before being qualified to take a national board exam and begin independent practice.[4] According to a 1988 study, the average diagnostic radiology resident sees 40 cases per day, or around 12,000 cases per year.[5] At the end of a residency, a diagnostic radiologist has acquired an average of 48,000 cases.

Psychologists and cognitive scientists agree that the time it takes to become an expert depends on the complexity of the task and the number of cases, or patterns, to which an individual is exposed. The more complex the task, the longer it takes to build expertise, or, more accurately, the longer it takes to experience a large number of cases or patterns.

The Power of Expertise

Experts are individuals with specialized knowledge suited to perform the specific tasks for which they are trained, but that expertise does not necessarily transfer to other domains.[6] A master chess player cannot apply chess expertise in a game of poker; although both chess and poker are games, a chess master who has never played poker is a novice poker player. Similarly, a biochemist is not qualified to perform neurosurgery, even though both biochemists and neurosurgeons study human physiology. In other words, the more complex a task, the more specialized and exclusive is the knowledge required to perform that task.

Experts perceive meaningful patterns in their domains better than do nonexperts. Where a novice perceives random or disconnected data points, an expert connects regular patterns within and among cases. This ability to identify patterns is not an innate perceptual skill; rather, it reflects the organization of knowledge after exposure to and experience with thousands of cases.[7]

Experts have a deeper understanding of their domains than do novices, and they utilize higher-order principles to solve problems.[8] A novice, for example, might group objects together by color or size, whereas an expert would group

---

[3] W. Chase and H. Simon, "Perception in Chess."

[4] American College of Radiology. Personal communication, 2002.

[5] A. Lesgold et al., "Expertise in a Complex Skill: Diagnosing X-Ray Pictures."

[6] M. Minsky and S. Papert, *Artificial Intelligence*; J. Voss and T. Post, "On the Solving of Ill-Structured Problems."

[7] O. Akin, *Models of Architectural Knowledge*; D. Egan and B. Schwartz, "Chunking in Recall of Symbolic Drawings"; K. McKeithen et al., "Knowledge Organization and Skill Differences in Computer Programmers."

the same objects according to their function or utility. Experts comprehend the meaning of data better than novices, and they weigh variables with different criteria within their domains better. Experts recognize variables that have the largest influence on a particular problem and focus their attention on those variables.

Experts have better domain-specific short-term and long-term memory than do novices.[9] Moreover, experts perform tasks in their domains faster than novices and commit fewer errors while solving problems.[10] Interestingly, experts also go about solving problems differently. At the beginning of a task, experts spend more time thinking about a problem than do novices, who immediately seek to find a solution.[11] Experts use their knowledge of previous cases as context for creating mental models to solve given problems.[12]

Because they are better at self-monitoring than novices, experts are more aware of instances where they have committed errors or failed to understand a problem.[13] They check their solutions more often and recognize when they are missing information necessary for solving a problem.[14] Experts are aware of the limits of their knowledge and apply their domain's heuristics to solve problems that fall outside of their experience base.

The Paradox of Expertise

The strengths of expertise can also be weaknesses.[15] Although one would expect experts to be good forecasters, they are not particularly good at it. Researchers have been testing the ability of experts to make forecasts since the 1930s.[16] The performance of experts has been tested against Bayesian probabilities to determine if they are better at making predictions than simple statistical models. Seventy years later, after more than 200 hundred experiments in different domains, it is clear that the answer is no.[17] Supplied with an equal amount of data about a particular case, Bayesian probability data are as

---

[8] M. Chi, P. Feltovich, and R. Glaser, "Categorization and Representation of Physics Problems by Experts and Novices"; M. Weiser and J. Shertz, "Programming Problem Representation in Novice and Expert Programmers."

[9] W. Chase and K. Ericsson, "Skill and Working Memory."

[10] W. Chase, "Spatial Representations of Taxi Drivers."

[11] J. Paige and H. Simon, "Cognition Processes in Solving Algebra Word Problems."

[12] Voss and Post.

[13] M. Chi, R. Glaser, and E. Rees, "Expertise in Problem Solving"; D. Simon and H. Simon, "Individual Differences in Solving Physics Problems."

[14] J. Larkin, "The Role of Problem Representation in Physics."

[15] C. Camerer and E. Johnson, "The Process-Performance Paradox in Expert Judgment."

[16] H. Reichenbach, *Experience and Prediction*; T. Sarbin, "A Contribution to the Study of Actuarial and Individual Methods of Prediction."

good as, or better than, an expert at making calls about the future. In fact, the expert does not tend to outperform the actuarial table, even if given more specific case information than is available to the statistical model.[18]

There are few exceptions to these research findings, but these are informative. When experts are given the results of the Bayesian probabilities, for example, they tend to score as well as the statistical model if they use the statistical information in making their own predictions.[19] In addition, if experts have privileged information that is not reflected in the statistical table, they will actually perform better than does the table. A classic example is the case of the judge's broken leg. Judge X has gone to the theater every Friday night for the past 10 years. Based on a Bayesian analysis, one would predict, with some certainty, that this Friday night would be no different. An expert knows, however, that the judge broke her leg Thursday afternoon and is expected to be in the hospital until Saturday. Knowing this key variable allows the expert to predict that the judge will not attend the theater this Friday.

Although having a single variable as the determining factor makes this case easy to grasp, analysis is seldom, if ever, this simple. Forecasting is a complex, interdisciplinary, dynamic, and multivariate task wherein many variables interact, weight and value change, and other variables are introduced or omitted.

During the past 30 years, researchers have categorized, experimented, and theorized about the cognitive aspects of forecasting and have sought to explain why experts are less accurate forecasters than statistical models. Despite such efforts, the literature shows little consensus regarding the causes or manifestations of human bias. Some have argued that experts, like all humans, are inconsistent when using mental models to make predictions. That is, the model an expert uses for predicting X in one month is different from the model used for predicting X in a later month, although precisely the same case and same data set are used in both instances.[20] A number of researchers point

---

[17] R. Dawes, D. Faust, and P. Meehl, "Clinical Versus Actuarial Judgment"; W. Grove and P. Meehl, "Comparative Efficiency of Informal (Subjective, Impressionistic) and Formal (Mechanical, Algorithmic) Prediction Procedures."

[18] R. Dawes, "A Case Study of Graduate Admissions"; Grove and Meehl; H. Sacks, "Promises, Performance, and Principles"; T. Sarbin, "A Contribution to the Study of Actuarial and Individual Methods of Prediction"; J. Sawyer, "Measurement and Prediction, Clinical and Statistical"; W. Schofield and J. Garrard, "Longitudinal Study of Medical Students Selected for Admission to Medical School by Actuarial and Committee Methods."

[19] L. Goldberg, "Simple Models or Simple Processes?"; L. Goldberg, "Man versus Model of Man"; D. Leli and S. Filskov, "Clinical-Actuarial Detection of and Description of Brain Impairment with the Wechsler-Bellevue Form I."

[20] J. Fries, et al., "Assessment of Radiologic Progression in Rheumatoid Arthritis."

to human biases to explain unreliable expert predictions.[21] There is general agreement that two types of bias exist:

- *Pattern bias*: looking for evidence that confirms rather than rejects a hypothesis and/or filling in—perhaps inadvertently—missing data with data from previous experiences;

- *Heuristic bias*: using inappropriate guidelines or rules to make predictions.

Paradoxically, the very method by which one becomes an expert explains why experts are much better than novices at describing, explaining, performing tasks, and solving problems within their domains but, with few exceptions, are worse at forecasting than are Bayesian probabilities based on historical, statistical models. A given domain has specific heuristics for performing tasks and solving problems, and these rules are a large part of what makes up expertise. In addition, experts need to acquire and store tens of thousands of cases in order to recognize patterns, generate and test hypotheses, and contribute to the collective knowledge within their fields. In other words, becoming an expert requires a significant number of years of viewing the world through the lens of one specific domain. This concentration gives the expert the power to recognize patterns, perform tasks, and solve problems, but it also focuses the expert's attention on one domain to the exclusion of others. It should come as little surprise, then, that an expert would have difficulty identifying and weighing variables in an interdisciplinary task, such as forecasting an adversary's intentions. Put differently, an expert may know his specific domain, such as economics or leadership analysis, quite thoroughly, but that may still not permit him to divine an adversary's intention, which the adversary may not himself know.

The Burden on Intelligence Analysts

Intelligence analysis is an amalgam of a number of highly specialized domains. Within each, experts are tasked with assembling, analyzing, assigning meaning to, and reporting on data, the goals being to describe an event or observation, solve a problem, or make a forecast. Experts who encounter a case outside their field repeat the steps they initially used to acquire their expertise. Thus, they can try to make the new data fit a pattern previously acquired; recognize that the case falls outside their expertise and turn to their domain's heuristics to try to give meaning to the data; acknowledge that the

---

[21] J. Evans, *Bias in Human Reasoning*; R. Heuer, *Psychology of Intelligence Analysis*; D. Kahneman, P. Slovic, and A. Tversky, *Judgment Under Uncertainty*; A. Tversky and D. Kahneman, "The Belief in the 'Law of Small Numbers'."

case still does not fit with their expertise and reject the data set as an anomaly; or consult other experts.

An item of information, in and of itself, is not domain specific. Imagine economic data that reveal that a country is investing in technological infrastructure, chemical supplies, and research and development. An economist might decide that the data fit an existing spending pattern and integrate these facts with prior knowledge about a country's economy. The same economist might decide that this is a new pattern that needs to be stored in long-term memory for some future use, or he might decide that the data are outliers of no consequence and may be ignored. Finally, the economist might decide that the data would be meaningful to a chemist or biologist and, therefore, seek to collaborate with other specialists, who might reach different conclusions regarding the data than would the economist.

In this example, the economist is required to use his economic expertise in all but the final option of consulting other experts. In the decision to seek collaboration, the economist is expected to know that what appears to be new economic data may have value to a chemist or biologist, domains with which he may have no experience. In other words, the economist is expected to know that an expert in some other field might find meaning in data that appear to be economic.

Three disparate variables complicate the economist's decisionmaking:

- *Time context.* This does not refer to the amount of time necessary to accomplish a task but rather to the limitations that come from being close to an event. The economist cannot say a priori that the new data set is *the* critical data set for some future event. In "real time," they are simply data to be manipulated. It is only in retrospect, or in long-term memory, that the economist can fit the data into a larger pattern, weigh their value, and assign them meaning.

- *Pattern bias.* In this particular example, the data have to do with infrastructure investment, and the expert is an economist. Thus, it makes perfect sense to try to manipulate the new data within the context of economics, recognizing, however, that there may be other, more important angles.

- *Heuristic bias.* The economist has spent a career becoming familiar with and using the guiding principles of economic analysis and, at best, has only a vague familiarity with other domains and their heuristics. An economist would not necessarily know that a chemist or biologist could identify what substance is being produced based on the types of equipment and supplies that are being purchased.

This example does not describe a complex problem; most people would recognize that the data from this case might be of value to other domains. It is one isolated case, viewed retrospectively, which could potentially affect two other domains. But, what if the economist had to deal with 100 data sets per day? Now, multiply those 100 data sets by the number of domains potentially interested in any given economic data set. Finally, put all of this in the context of "real time." The economic expert is now expected to maintain expertise in economics, which is a full-time endeavor, while simultaneously acquiring some level of experience in every other domain. Based on these expectations, the knowledge requirements for effective collaboration quickly exceed the capabilities of the individual expert.

The expert is left dealing with all of these data through the lens of his own expertise. Let's assume that he uses his domain heuristics to incorporate the data into an existing pattern, store the data in long-term memory as a new pattern, or reject the data set as an outlier. In each of these options, the data stop with the economist instead of being shared with an expert in some other domain. The fact that these data are not shared then becomes a potentially critical case of analytic error.[22]

In hindsight, critics will say that the implications were obvious—that the crisis could have been avoided if the data had been passed to one or another specific expert. In "real time," however, an expert often does not know which particular data set would have value for an expert in another domain.

The Pros and Cons of Teams

One obvious solution to the paradox of expertise is to assemble an interdisciplinary team. Why not simply make all problem areas or country-specific data available to a team of experts from a variety of domains? This ought, at least, to reduce the pattern and heuristic biases inherent in relying on only one domain. Ignoring potential security issues, there are practical problems with this approach. First, each expert would have to sift through large data sets to find data specific to his expertise. This would be inordinately time-consuming and might not even be routinely possible, given the priority accorded gisting and current reporting.

Second, during the act of scanning large data sets, the expert inevitably would be looking for data that fit within his area of expertise. Imagine a chemist who comes across data that show that a country is investing in technologi-

---

[22] L. Kirkpatrick, *Captains Without Eyes: Intelligence Failures in World War II*; F. Shiels, *Preventable Disasters*; J. Wirtz, *The Tet Offensive: Intelligence Failure in War*; R. Wohlstetter, *Pearl Harbor.*

cal infrastructure, chemical supplies, and research and development (the same data that the economist analyzed in the previous example). The chemist recognizes that these are the ingredients necessary for a nation to produce a specific chemical agent, which could have a military application or could be benign. The chemist then meshes the data with an existing pattern, stores the data as a new pattern, or ignores the data as an anomaly.

The chemist, however, has no frame of reference regarding spending trends in the country of interest. He does not know if the investment in chemical supplies represents an increase, a decrease, or a static spending pattern—answers the economist could supply immediately. There is no reason for the chemist to know if a country's ability to produce this chemical agent is a new phenomenon. Perhaps the country in question has been producing the chemical agent for years, and these data are part of some normal pattern of behavior.

If this analytic exercise is to begin to coalesce, neither expert must treat the data set as an anomaly and both must report it as significant. In addition, each expert's analysis of the data—an increase in spending and the identification of a specific chemical agent—must be brought together at some point. The problem is, at what point? Presumably, someone will get both of these reports somewhere along the intelligence chain. Of course, the individual who gets these reports will be subject to the same three complicating variables described earlier—time context, pattern bias, and heuristic bias—and may not be able to synthesize the information. Thus, the burden of putting the pieces together will merely have been shifted to someone else in the organization.

In order to avoid shifting the problem from one expert to another, an actual collaborative team could be built. Why not explicitly put the economist and the chemist together to work on analyzing data? The utilitarian problems with this strategy are obvious: not all economic problems are chemical, and not all chemical problems are economic. Each expert would waste an inordinate amount of time. Perhaps one case in 100 would be applicable to both experts, but, during the rest of the day, they would drift back to their individual domains, in part, because that is what they are best at and, in part, just to stay busy.

Closer to the real world, the same example may also have social, political, historical, and cultural aspects. Despite an increase in spending on a specific chemical agent, the country in question may not be inclined to use it in a threatening way. For example, there may be social data unavailable to the economist or the chemist indicating that the chemical agent will be used for a benign purpose. In order for collaboration to work, each team would have to have experts from many domains working together on the same data set.

Successful teams have very specific organizational and structural requirements. An effective team requires discrete and clearly stated goals that are shared by each team member.[23] Teams also require interdependence and accountability, that is, the success of each individual depends on the success of the team as a whole as well as on the individual success of every other team member.[24]

Effective teams require cohesion, formal and informal communication, cooperation, shared mental models, and similar knowledge structures.[25] Putting combinations such as this in place is not a trivial task. Creating shared mental models may be fairly easy within an air crew or a tank crew, where an individual's role is clearly identifiable as part of a clearly-defined, repetitive team effort, such as landing a plane or acquiring and firing on a target. It is more difficult within an intelligence team, given the vague nature of the goals, the enormity of the task, and the diversity of individual expertise. Moreover, the larger the number of team members, the more difficult it is to generate cohesion, communication, and cooperation. Heterogeneity can also be a challenge; it has a positive effect on generating diverse viewpoints within a team, but it requires more organizational structure than does a homogeneous team.[26]

Without specific processes, organizing principles, and operational structures, interdisciplinary teams will quickly revert to being simply a room full of experts who ultimately drift back to their previous work patterns. That is, the experts will not be a team at all; they will be a group of experts individually working in some general problem space.[27]

---

[23] Dorwin Cartwright and Alvin Zander, *Group Dynamics: Research and Theory*; P. Fandt, W. Richardson, and H. Conner, "The Impact of Goal Setting on Team Simulation Experience"; J. Harvey and C. Boettger, "Improving Communication within a Managerial Workgroup."

[24] M. Deutsch, "The Effects of Cooperation and Competition Upon Group Process"; D. Johnson and R. Johnson, "The Internal Dynamics of Cooperative Learning Groups"; D. Cartwright and A. Zander, *Group Dynamics: Research and Theory;* David Johnson and Roger Johnson, "The Internal Dynamics of Cooperative Learning Groups"; D. Johnson et al., "Effects of Cooperative, Competitive, and Individualistic Goal Structure on Achievement: A Meta-Analysis"; R. Slavin, "Research on Cooperative Learning"; R. Slavin, *Cooperative Learning.*

[25] J. Cannon-Bowers, E. Salas, S. Converse, "Shared Mental Models in Expert Team Decision Making"; L. Coch and J. French, "Overcoming Resistance to Change"; M. Deutsch, "The Effects of Cooperation and Competition Upon Group Process"; L. Festinger, "Informal Social Communication"; D. Johnson et al., "The Impact of Positive Goal and Resource Interdependence on Achievement, Interaction, and Attitudes"; B. Mullen and C. Copper, "The Relation Between Group Cohesiveness and Performance: An Integration"; W. Nijhof and P. Kommers, "An Analysis of Cooperation in Relation to Cognitive Controversy"; J. Orasanu, "Shared Mental Models and Crew Performance"; S. Seashore, *Group Cohesiveness in the Industrial Work-group.*

[26] T. Mills, "Power Relations in Three-Person Groups"; L. Molm, "Linking Power Structure and Power Use"; V. Nieva, E. Fleishman, and A. Rieck, *Team Dimensions: Their Identity, Their Measurement, and Their Relationships*; G. Simmel, *The Sociology of Georg Simmel.*

[27] R. Johnston, *Decision Making and Performance Error in Teams: Research Results*; J. Meister, "Individual Perceptions of Team Learning Experiences Using Video-Based or Virtual Reality Environments."

Can Technology Help?

There are potential technological alternatives to multifaceted teams. For example, an Electronic Performance Support System (EPSS) is a large database that is used in conjunction with expert systems, intelligent agents, and decision aids.[28] Although applying such a system to intelligence problems might be a useful goal, at present, the notion of an integrated EPSS for large complex data sets is more theory than practice.[29] In addition to questions about the technological feasibility of such a system, there are fundamental epistemological challenges. It is virtually inconceivable that a comprehensive computational system could bypass the three complicating variables of expertise described earlier.

An EPSS, or any other computational solution, is designed, programmed, and implemented by a human expert from one domain only, that of computer science. Historians will not design the "historical decision aid," economists will not program the "economic intelligent agent," chemists will not create the "chemical agent expert system." Computer scientists may consult with various experts during the design phase of such a system, but, when it is time to sit down and write code, the programmer will follow the heuristics with which he is familiar.[30] In essence, one would be trading the heuristics of dozens of domains for those that govern computer science. This would reduce the problem of processing time by simplifying and linking data, and it might reduce pattern bias. It would not reduce heuristic bias, however; if anything, it might exaggerate it by reducing all data to a binary state.[31]

This skepticism is not simply a Luddite reaction to technology. Computational systems have had a remarkable, positive effect on processing time, storage, and retrieval. They have also demonstrated utility in identifying patterns within narrowly defined domains. However, intelligence analysis requires the expertise of so many diverse fields of study and is not something a computational system handles well. Although an EPSS, or some other form of computational system, may be a useful tool for manipulating data, it is not a solution to the paradox of expertise.

---

[28] An *Expert System* is a job-specific heuristic process that helps an expert narrow the range of available choices. An *Intelligent Agent* is an automated program (bot) with built-in heuristics used in Web searches. A *Decision Aid* is an expert system whose scope is limited to a particular task.

[29] R. Johnston, "Electronic Performance Support Systems and Information Navigation."

[30] R. Johnston and J. Fletcher, *A Meta-Analysis of the Effectiveness of Computer-Based Training for Military Instruction.*

[31] J. Fletcher and R. Johnston, "Effectiveness and Cost Benefits of Computer-Based Decision Aids for Equipment Maintenance."

Analytic Methodologists

Most domains have specialists who study the scientific process or research methods of their discipline. Instead of specializing in a specific substantive topic, these experts specialize in mastering the research and analytic methods of their domain. In the biological and medical fields, these methodological specialists are epidemiologists. In education and public policy, they are program evaluators. In other fields, they are research methodologists or statisticians. Whatever the label, each field recognizes that it requires experts in methodology who focus on deriving meaning from data, recognizing patterns, and solving problems within a domain in order to maintain and pass on the domain's heuristics. They become in-house consultants—organizing agents—who work to identify research designs, methods for choosing samples, and tools for data analysis.

Because they have a different perspective than do the experts in a domain, methodologists are often called on by substantive experts to advise them on a variety of process issues. On any given day, an epidemiologist, for example, may be asked to consult on studies of the effects of alcoholism or the spread of a virus on a community or to review a double-blind clinical trial of a new pharmaceutical product. In each case, the epidemiologist is not being asked about the content of the study; rather, he is being asked to comment on the research methods and data analysis techniques used.

Although well over 160 analytic methods are available to intelligence analyst, few methods specific to the domain of intelligence analysis exist.[32] Intelligence analysis has few specialists whose professional training is in the process of employing and unifying the analytic practices within the field. It is left to the individual analysts to know how to apply methods, select one method over another, weigh disparate variables, and synthesize the results—the same analysts whose expertise is confined to specific substantive areas and their own domains' heuristics.

Conclusion

Intelligence agencies continue to experiment with the right composition, structure, and organization of analytic teams. Yet, although they budget significant resources for technological solutions, comparatively little is being

---

[32] Exceptions include: S. Feder, "FACTIONS and Policon"; R. Heuer, *Psychology of Intelligence Analysis*; R. Hopkins, *Warnings of Revolution: A Case Study of El Salvador*; J. Lockwood and K. Lockwood, "The Lockwood Analytical Method for Prediction (LAMP)"; J. Pierce, "Some Mathematical Methods for Intelligence Analysis"; E. Sapp, "Decision Trees"; J. Zlotnick, "Bayes' Theorem for Intelligence Analysis."

done to advance methodological science. Methodological improvements are left primarily to the individual domains, a practice that risks falling into the same paradoxical trap that currently exists. What is needed is an intelligence-centric approach to methodology that will include the methods and procedures of many domains and the development of heuristics and techniques unique to intelligence. In short, intelligence analysis needs its own analytic heuristics that are designed, developed, and tested by professional analytic methodologists.

The desired outcome would be a combined approach that includes formal thematic teams with structured organizational principles, technological systems designed with significant input from domain experts, and a cadre of analytic methodologists. These methodologists would act as in-house consultants for analytic teams, generate new methods specific to intelligence analysis, modify and improve existing methods of analysis, and promote the professionalization of the discipline of intelligence. Although, at first, developing a cadre of analytic methodologists would require using specialists from a variety of other domains and professional associations, in time, the discipline would mature into its own subdiscipline with its own measures of validity and reliability.

CHAPTER SIX

The Question of Foreign Cultures: Combating Ethnocentrism in Intelligence Analysis

The intelligence literature often cautions intelligence professionals to be wary of mirror imaging.[1] Although the term is a misnomer (a mirror image is a reverse image), the concept is that individuals perceive foreigners—both friends and adversaries of the United States—as thinking the same way as Americans.[2] Individuals do, in fact, have a natural tendency to assume that others think and perceive the world in the same way they do. This type of projective identification, or ethnocentrism, is the consequence of a combination of cognitive and cultural biases resulting from a lifetime of enculturation, culturally bound heuristics, and missing, or inadequate, information.[3]

Ethnocentrism is a phenomenon that operates on a conscious level, but it is difficult to recognize in oneself and equally difficult to counteract. In part, this is because, in cases of ethnocentric thinking, an individual does not recognize that important information is missing or, more important, that his worldview and problem-solving heuristics interfere with the process of recognizing information that conflicts or refutes his assumptions.

Take, for example, the proposition that others do not think like Americans. It seems only intuitive that other tribes, ethnic groups, nationalities, and states

---

[1] Alexander Butterfield, *The Accuracy of Intelligence Assessment;* Richards J. Heuer, Jr., *Psychology of Intelligence Analysis*; Lisa Krizan, *Intelligence Essentials for Everyone*; J. R. Thompson, R. Hopf-Weichel, and R. Geiselman, *The Cognitive Bases of Intelligence Analysis.*

[2] In this work, I use the broader term "ethnocentrism" to refer to the concept represented by mirror imaging and projective identification .

[3] In anthropology, ethnocentrism is the tendency to judge the customs of other societies by the standards of one's own culture. This includes projecting one's own cognition and norms onto others.

have different histories, languages, customs, educational practices, and cultures and, therefore, must think differently from one another.

The problem, however, is that the cognitive process of understanding or even recognizing that there are cultural and cognitive differences is not intuitive at all. Intuition is the act of immediate cognition, that is, perceiving something directly through the use of culturally dependent heuristics and cognitive patterns accumulated through a lifetime without requiring the use of rational or formal processes. This effort appears doomed to failure, because "trying to think like them" all too often results in applying the logic of one's own culture and experience to try to understand the actions of others, without knowing that one is using the logic of one's own culture. This, however, does not have to be the case. Through acculturation and the use of specific strategies, tools, and techniques, it is possible to combat the effects of ethnocentrism without trying to "think like them." This text includes two short case studies on failures to recognize ethnocentrism, both drawn from the author's own experience and told from his perspective. These failures are then examined with the goal of developing strategies and techniques to combat ethnocentric bias.

Case Study One: Tiananmen Square

At the time of the prodemocracy protests of the Chinese students and, to a lesser extent, workers, between April and June of 1989, I too was a college student. I mention this because American college students and Chinese college students tend to perceive themselves in very different ways, and they are perceived by their societies as having very different social roles. Chinese students perceive themselves as having moral authority, and they are perceived as controlling social capital and possessing public status. There is a cultural norm in China that students, as the future elite, have a morally superior role in society. I remember thinking at the time that, with the obvious exception of those in power, who risked losing their privileged positions, any "right-minded" person in China would support democracy. A movement for democratic reform would liberalize the policies of a repressive regime, encourage personal freedom, and give the Chinese people a voice in their lives.

When the university students went on strike and took over Tiananmen Square, the popular view in the United States, reflected in the US media, was that they were college students protesting for democratic reform. There were images of thousands of students rallying and camping out on and around the statue of the People's Heroes. Throughout the square, banners and posters from universities supported democracy and freedom. The statue of the Goddess of Democracy erected by the demonstrators looked very much like our Statue of Liberty. Labor groups offered to join the students, people paraded in front of the Great Hall of the People, and citizens donated blankets and food.

Student leaders began a hunger strike to force a dialogue between the students and the government. All signs seemed clearly to point to a popular movement for democracy, for which there was a groundswell of support.

The Chinese government seemed hesitant or unsure. The People's Liberation Army (PLA) was sent to surround the square, but citizens blocked their advance and tried to persuade the troops to be neutral. A curfew order was not obeyed; martial law was declared and ignored. Another PLA move on Tiananmen Square was repelled. It appeared that the students had forced a stalemate and that their demands would be heard.

At that point, my assumption was that the government was weakened and would be forced to respond to the protesters' demands, at least to some degree. I anticipated a dialogue and concessions on both sides. Although I imagined the government was capable of resorting to violence, I assumed that it would not. It seemed inconceivable that the citizens of Beijing—10–12 million people—would not intervene on behalf of the students. That many people could have overwhelmed the PLA had they chosen to do so. I also assumed that the soldiers of the PLA would be reluctant to fire on their own people, partly because the majority of both groups were from the same, dominant ethnic group of China, the Han, and, in part, because the soldiers represented a lower rung of Chinese society then did the students. The notion of soldiers killing students would be an affront to the sensibilities of the Han, or so I thought. I was wrong.

In the end, when the PLA carried out its orders to clear the square with force and end the protest, support for the protesters turned out to be relatively slight. The Chinese "middle class" never came to the students' aid; the great majority of the Beijing populace simply watched the events unfold. Moreover, it turned out that the labor groups participating in the demonstration were actually protesting against corporate corruption and the lack of job stability brought about by market reforms and not in support of the students' demands for a loosening of restrictions on expression. What I perceived to be a groundswell of popular support for the students had been exaggerated and wishful thinking on my part.

My failure to anticipate the way events would actual unfold in Tiananmen Square was tied to ethnocentric thinking and a lack of accurate and contextual information. Students in the United States are encouraged to be politically active, and their protests are often seen merely as minor inconveniences that need to be endured. In China, however, the protesting students were seen as a direct challenge to political authority and, much more so than in the United States, their actions were viewed as an outright conflict between the future elite and the current leadership. The protest itself was viewed as a violation of a taboo, upsetting the cultural order and the stability of society.

As an observer, I missed the cultural context that was necessary to view the events as an actual conflict and could not convince myself that a violent solution was a possibility. I had discounted the hypothesis that violence would occur, because I could not imagine it occurring in the United States. This led me to discount raw data that would have refuted a hypothesis that the two factions would reach a compromise. In addition, at that time, I had no formal grounding in Chinese studies, nor had I been to China. Thus, I had not acquired information that would have helped me create a meaningful context for the event.

Years later, my wife and I were in China doing ethnographic fieldwork on the socioeconomic effects of the spread of the English language and American culture in urban and rural China.[4] While there, we spent a great deal of time talking with others about the events of Tiananmen, and we decided to include in our research questions about the student protests, if for no other reason than to satisfy our own curiosity.

What we found stood in contrast to media reports and the opinions expressed by many pundits and scholars in the US and the West. After hundreds of interviews with a wide variety of people in and around Beijing, we found a consistent preoccupation among the "silent majority." That was the Cultural Revolution, which had affected all of the people we interviewed. They had been participants, observers, or survivors, and, often, all three.

In the mid-1960s, Mao Zedong sought to recapture power from reform-minded opponents within the Communist Party. Using radical party leaders as his instruments, he created the Red Guard, which was made up primarily of college students (although others followed suit in time). The image of the Cultural Revolution was not simply the image of Mao; it was also the image of angry, violent, and powerful college students, who were the most visible proponents of the "Cult of Mao." According to the people we interviewed, it was the students who had chanted slogans, raised banners, paraded in public spaces, resisted older forms of social control, and seized power. With that power and the blessings of Mao, the youth and university students had committed many of the atrocities of the Cultural Revolution and plunged China into a decade of chaos, during which many institutions, including schools, were closed and many of the country's cultural and historical artifacts were destroyed.

---

[4] American anthropology is based on the ethnographic method and direct interaction with the people who are being studied. This interaction includes direct and participant observation and interviews, or fieldwork, where one lives with the people being investigated. Continental European schools of anthropology are not as obsessed with methodology and hands-on experience and tend to the more theoretical.

At the height of the Cultural Revolution, any dissent was sufficient to bring accusations of counterrevolutionary sympathies and to qualify one for "re-education," which could mean public denunciation, job loss, incarceration, forced labor, relocation, and even murder, torture, and rape. The traditional values of respect and honor were replaced with violence and terror, and the historical social unit of the family had been disrupted and replaced with the cult of Mao.

For those who had lived through the Cultural Revolution, the student challenge to the government in Tiananmen in 1989 was also a challenge to social order and stability. The people we interviewed remembered, correctly or not, that the faction of the Communist Party then in power and the PLA had stopped the Red Guard and the Cultural Revolution, arrested its highest ranking proponents and beneficiaries, the Gang of Four, and eventually restored order to the nation. The point of view of the people we interviewed was that the PLA, despite the low social status of soldiers, had stopped the chaos. Although they did not approve of killing students, the threat of another cultural revolution, democratic or otherwise, was more disturbing to them than the bloody climax in the square. Social order was the higher virtue.

Tiananmen Square: Discussion

We cut nature up, organize it into concepts, and ascribe significances as we do, largely because we are parties to an agreement to organize it in this way—an agreement that holds throughout our speech community and is codified in the patterns of our language.

Benjamin Whorf[5]

In 1987, a Chinese academic, Min Qi, performed the first national survey of Chinese political culture.[6] Respondents were asked, among other things, to select statements that best described their understanding of democracy. Of the 1,373 respondents, 6.6 percent responded that democracy meant that people could elect their political leaders and 3.4 percent that power was limited and divided. These replies tended to be from individuals under 25 years of age, in college, and living in urban centers.

---

[5] Benjamin Whorf, along with fellow anthropologist Edward Sapir, developed the linguistic relativity hypothesis, asserting that different speech communities had different patterns of thought. Although challenged by linguist/philosopher Noam Chomsky and others with the Universal Grammar hypothesis, linguistic relativity still has a significant amount of empirical research support. Benjamin Whorf, *Language, Thought, and Reality.*

[6] Min Qi, *Zhongguo Zhengzhi Wenhua* [Chinese Political Culture]. Translation courtesy of a friend of the author who prefers to remain anonymous.

In contrast, 25 percent responded that democracy was guided by the center (the party and the cadres), 19.5 percent that democracy meant that the government would solicit people's opinions (the party would ask people what they thought), and 11 percent that democracy meant the government would make decisions for the people based on the people's interests but not including the people's direct vote. These three responses were more in line with then-current party doctrine and tended to be from individuals over 36 years of age living in both urban and rural settings. This was the same demographic that experienced the Cultural Revolution.

The election of representatives and the division and limitation of those representatives' power—what I would have considered to be two key aspects of democracy—were chosen by 10 percent of the sample, only slightly larger than the 6.3 percent of Chinese respondents who reported that they didn't know what the word "democracy" meant. My own perception of democracy fit with a young, urban, elite, college educated population, not with the majority of Chinese citizens.

There was a very small sample of citizens in Tiananmen Square demanding what looked and sounded like my American version of democracy. Yet, however much the students' message resonated in the West, it did not do so in China. My expectations notwithstanding, there was a cognitive disconnect between students and average citizens, which, along with the visceral semiotics of the Cultural Revolution, kept the two apart.[7] It was not just the message that had kept people in their homes during the PLA siege on Tiananmen; it was also the messengers.

The label "ethnocentrism" might be accurate, but it does not diagnose the root of the problem. I did not use a variety of tools or techniques to question my underlying assumptions and, therefore, I failed to make an accurate forecast. There were obvious statistical and analytic flaws. The former was principally a sampling error, both frame and selection bias (the students at Tiananmen did not represent the general population in Beijing or China at large). More significant than simple technical or statistical flaws, however, my frame of reference and my assumptions about meanings, context, and values (or culture) misled me.

The assumptions I made about the Tiananmen protests were products of my own enculturation, and I am not convinced that anything short of the experience of analytic failure would have been sufficient for me to examine the process underpinning my reasoning. I never would have reexamined my mental mode without experiencing failure. Failure is an event that is easily remem-

---

[7] Semiosis is the production of cultural signifiers or signs and the cultural or contextual meaning of those signs. This includes all modes of visual and auditory production.

bered; it affects the ego and drives one to investigate errors and to adapt or change behavior based on those investigations. Failure is a learning event and results in a teachable moment.[8]

There seems to be little reason to perform a postmortem when events unfold as predicted. The natural assumption is that the mechanisms of analysis were valid, because the results of the analysis were accurate. The obvious danger is that this assumption discounts the possibility that one may be accurate purely by accident. Moreover, by focusing only on failure, one risks sampling bias by only choosing cases in which there was error. The risk of ignoring success is that potential lessons may go undiscovered. An alternative to relying on failure to challenge one's assumptions is to create a standard practice of reviewing each case regardless of outcome, principally through the use of a formal After Action Review (AAR).

Case Study Two: The Red Team

Recently, I was asked to serve on a newly formed red team within the Department of Defense. I agreed to participate, despite a number of serious concerns having to do both with the nature and structure of red teams in general and with my own experience with ethnocentrism and its effects on analysis. These concerns are applicable not only to red teams, but also to any analyst put in the position of trying to "think like them."[9]

This particular red team was part of a constructive/conceptual war game in which there were 11 participants, seven of whom had doctorates. Of the seven doctorates, three were psychologists, one was a historian, one was an economist, one was a political scientist, and one was an anthropologist. The other four participants had extensive military backgrounds. There were no physical scientists or engineers. Nine of the 11 participants were white males, one was a male born in the region of interest, and one was a white female. All were middle class. Seven of the 11 were raised in nominally Christian homes and three in nominally Jewish homes. (I say nominally because it was not possible to determine their level of religious commitment during this exercise.)

I mention the demographics of the group because it was not representative of the adversary we were intended to simulate. Although the group had

---

[8] Charles Perrow, *Normal Accidents.*

[9] Military red teams are meant to simulate the actions of an adversary in some type of war game or crisis simulation, usually with the goal of generating scenarios for training and readiness or for logistics and planning. These war games may be *live*, e.g., force-on-force simulations like those of the US Army Combat Training Centers; *virtual*, as in flight simulators; or *constructive*, either digital theater-level simulations or purely conceptual games centered on strategic, tactical, or operational issues.

numerous domain matter experts, very few had first-hand knowledge of the region of interest. Only one participant was from the area, had spent formative years there, spoke the languages, and experienced the culture firsthand. As this group was assembled to simulate the behavior and decisionmaking of a foreign adversary, this aspect was more important than it would have been for a substantive team developing threat assessments around a specific topic or target. Consequently, the scenarios developed by the red team often reflected an adversary whose behavior and decisionmaking resembled those of educated, white, middle class Americans.

The one member of the red team who had been born in and spent formative years in the region of interest regularly stopped the scenario development process by saying, "They wouldn't do that" or "They don't think that way." On several occasions, he objected, "This scenario is way too complex" or "They wouldn't use that tactic; it requires too much direct communication." His objections were not usually based on military considerations; rather, they were based on the cultural norms and mores of the adversary. He talked of kinship relationships as a specific type of social network in the region and of the value of kinship for understanding the adversary's intentions. In short, he brought an ethnographic perspective to the exercise.

Having no personal or professional experience with this region or its cultures, I thought it appropriate to defer to his first-person experience. Ultimately, however, it proved difficult to convince the group that this man's cultural knowledge was, in fact, an area of specialized knowledge that needed to be factored into each scenario. This difficulty was born out of another type of ethnocentric bias.

Inviting an anthropologist to a red team exercise presupposes that the red team takes seriously the notion that cultural differences matter and that those cultural factors ought to be made explicit in the analytic process. The problem in this case was that the anthropologist was not an area expert for this region and its cultures, and the one area expert who was there lacked the academic credentials to be taken seriously by the other members of the group. Had I been able to assert the same concepts that the other individual asserted, it would have had a certain academic, or scientific, imprimatur because of my training and experience. Because he lacked these credentials, many of the other individual's insights were lost, and the analytic product suffered as a result.

The Red Team: Discussion

I am reluctant to fault the organizers for the ethnocentric bias in the demographic composition of the red team. It is very difficult to assemble a truly representative red team. There is the obvious problem of security. Someone fully able to represent the adversary culturally would very likely be unable to obtain requisite clearances for participation in a classified red team exercise. In fact, even if it were possible to find someone both culturally representative *and* sympathetic to the goals of the red team, such as the participant born in the region, the conflicts triggered by that sympathy, cultural identity, and cultural allegiance could well lead to unforeseen cognitive biases that would be difficult to counteract.[10]

An alternative is to find an ethnic American citizen with similarities to the people of the region of interest, but simply finding a US citizen with the same ethnicity as those of the region of interest does not guarantee any special insight into their thinking. Ethnicity is not the same as sharing culture or identity. Not all ethnic groups in the US are isolated and self-perpetuating. Many, in fact, put great effort into trying to assimilate into the larger "American culture" by distancing themselves from their culture of origin. These people often struggle with their own concept of cultural identity and the broader issues of community affiliation.[11] Many immigrants and most first-generation offspring have already begun the process of acculturation. More striking, their offspring display a process of enculturation in the US by learning the language, attending the schools, assimilating local and national values, and establishing ties to a diverse community outside of their own ethnic enclave. In fact, the children of recent immigrants share many of the same cognitive filters as those who are generations removed from migration. That said, there are American citizens born in the region of interest, like the member of the red team in which I participated, who do have insight into specific cultures, principally because their enculturation was affected by being born in, and living in, a foreign region.

The participant in that red team was a foreign-born American citizen, but foreign birth is not a necessary condition for enculturation.[12] Living in a foreign region, speaking the language, interacting with the people, developing community ties, and establishing an identity within that community are all part of the acculturation process and allow one to alter the cognitive filters through which one interprets the world. Time spent on a US military base, in a US embassy, or in a Western hotel overseas does not lead to acculturation.

---

[10] Philip Cushman, *Constructing the Self, Constructing America*; John Lucy, *Language Diversity and Thought*; Douglass Price-Williams, *Explorations in Cross-Cultural Psychology*; Marshall Segall, *Cross-Cultural Psychology*; Richard Shweder, *Thinking Through Cultures*; Yali Zou and Enrique Trueba, *Ethnic Identity and Power*; and Benjamin Whorf.

[11] David Levinson and Melvin Ember, *American Immigrant Cultures*. For raw data covering 186 cultural groups since 1937, including immigrants, see the Human Relations Area Files at Yale University.

[12] Some anthropologists have argued that enculturation is specific to childhood but the evidence supports that it is a lifelong process. See Segall.

Quite the contrary, each of these is a "virtual" America, an approximation of life in the United States on some foreign soil, and it is the time spent away from these institutions that is important.

The red team experience reinforced lessons I learned from my own analytic failures and biases. Watching the struggle between the man enculturated in the region of interest and the academic experts was a frustrating experience. It was clear that the experts would not, or could not, hear what he was saying and that neither he nor I knew how to get the other experts to listen. I doubt this communication failure was the result of stubbornness or arrogance on anyone's part. It seemed rather that the experts' thinking naturally defaulted to their own cultural reference points, which interfered with his attempts to communicate his cultural knowledge.

Specific cultural knowledge is a skill and the foundation for forecasting the behavior and decisionmaking of foreign actors. Acquiring cultural knowledge should be taken as seriously as learning any other facet of one's analytic capabilities. Moreover, it is incumbent on analysts to educate their own leadership and policymakers about the value and utility of cultural knowledge for intelligence analysis.

Conclusion and Recommendations

Ethnocentrism is a normal condition, and it results in analytic bias. The analytic community and intelligence researchers need to develop tools and techniques to combat analytic ethnocentrism. I believe that using cultural diversity as a strategy to combat ethnocentrism has much to recommend it. [13]

Security concerns may make it very difficult, if not impossible, to hire people who are genuinely representative of a given culture. As an alternative to focusing on hiring practices, I recommend a formal cultural training program to facilitate acculturation. The program would include language acquisition and a classroom segment centered on specific cultures, but it would go beyond these by having the students go to countries of interest and interact with the

---

[13] Some social action groups have appropriated the words "cultural diversity" from Levi-Strauss and the French school of structural anthropology as a rallying cry to advance an agenda of equal access to resources and power. That is, the concept has been politicized, and, invoking the words "cultural diversity" in a public forum ensures that people will have some emotional reaction. This is not my intention. The use of the words in this work is meant strictly in the technical sense, specifically, that is, to refer to individuals whose enculturation occurs among different cultures or individuals who have experienced acculturation. Acculturation is not specific to any one group, all people can and do experience acculturation to one degree or another through cultural contact and cultural diffusion, defined as the spreading of a cultural trait (e.g., material object, idea, or behavior pattern) from one society to another without wholesale dislocation or migration. Moreover, acculturation can be accomplished purposefully through training and fieldwork.

people in their own setting and on their own terms. Students would be encouraged to investigate the rituals, norms, taboos, kinship systems, and social networks of the cultures being studied. There would also be provision for continuing on-line education and an on-line community of practice for mentoring, problem solving, and peer-to-peer interaction.

In my view, a stand-alone training program would be insufficient to affect analytic processes without specific follow-on programs. Retention of training requires repetition, problem solving, application, and evaluation. People must use what they learn and then determine if what they have learned can improve the quality of their work. To this end, I recommend a formal After Action Review (AAR) process.

The AAR is used by the US Army to capture lessons learned after a training exercise or a live operation. Unlike conventional postmortems and traditional performance critiques, the AAR is used to evaluate successes as well as failures. Although failure generally receives more scrutiny and attention than success, an approach that only examines failure results in sampling error. If one only scrutinizes mistakes, otherwise effective methods may be blamed for the errors. That those techniques were successful in 99 out of 100 cases can go unnoticed, with the result that the failures receive disproportionate attention and bias the statistical results of the postmortem. The AAR was specifically designed to avoid this problem.

The AAR process was introduced in the mid 1970s, but it is based on the oral history method of "after combat interviews" employed by S.L.A. Marshall during World War II, the Korean War, and the Vietnam War. As soon as possible after a battle, regardless of the outcome, Marshall would assemble soldiers who were involved and, using a semistructured interview technique, would engage them in a group discussion about their individual and team roles and actions during combat.

The current AAR method also includes such objective data as tactics, logistics, kill ratios, time-to-task, accuracy-of-task, and operational outcomes.[14] Informed by the objective data, a group discussion led by a facilitator trained in the elicitation process ensues. The AAR, along with supporting documents, such as historical studies and relevant doctrinal materials, is then stored in a knowledge repository at the US Army's Center for Army Lessons Learned (CALL).[15]

With some customization, an AAR process and a lessons learned repository could be created for intelligence analysts. Although seemingly time-consuming and cumbersome, with training and expert facilitators, the AAR process could be modified and streamlined for use by analysts at the end of a production cycle. As

---

[14] John Morrison and Larry Meliza, *Foundations of the After Action Review Process.*

a practical matter, the process would be used mostly with longer works, such as assessments or estimates. The intelligence product, along with AAR notes, would then be incorporated in a community knowledge repository. This knowledge repository would also help in the development and refinement of advanced analytic courses by providing course developers with baseline analytic data. In short, the repository becomes a tool for continuous educational needs analysis and links training directly to the actual work practices of analysts. These data can be used as a test bed for research on the effectiveness of analytic methodology. In this way, the lessons learned are not lost to future generations of analysts.

---

[15] See the US Army Center for Army Lessons Learned Web site, which has links to numerous other repositories. Although each organization has customized the concept to meet its unique needs, all of the US military services, the National Aeronautics and Space Administration, the Department of Energy, the Environmental Protection Agency, the North Atlantic Treaty Organization, the United Nations, and the ministries of defense of Australia and Canada, currently have Lessons Learned repositories.

CHAPTER SEVEN

Instructional Technology: Effectiveness and Implications for the Intelligence Community

J. D. Fletcher[1]
Rob Johnston

The Intelligence Community has begun to invest substantial resources in the training and education of its analysts. With the exception of a few advanced courses available through distance learning networks, this instruction is delivered using a conventional classroom model. This model possesses a number of inherent inefficiencies, including inconsistent instruction, strict ties to time and place of instruction, large student-to-instructor ratios, and limited active participation by students due to class size and scheduling.

Research suggests that significant improvements can be achieved through the use of computer-based instructional technology. According to these studies, this technology can increase instructional effectiveness and reduce time needed to learn. It can achieve these efficiencies, moreover, while both lowering the cost of instruction and increasing its availability.[2] This chapter summarizes evidence on the promise of instructional technology for intelligence analysis training.

---

[1] Dr. J. D. Fletcher is a research staff member at the Institute for Defense Analyses, where he specializes in issues of manpower, personnel, and training. He holds graduate degrees in computer science and educational psychology from Stanford University.

[2] Because instructional technology makes few distinctions between formal education and professional training, the term "instruction" will be used for both in this chapter.

Background

The argument for the use of instructional technology usually begins with a comparative examination of the effectiveness of classroom instruction and individual tutoring. For instance, the graph below illustrates the combined findings of three dissertation studies that compared one-on-one tutoring with one-on-many classroom instruction.[3]

It is not surprising that such comparisons would show that tutored students learned more than those taught in classrooms. What is surprising is the magnitude of the difference. Overall, as the figure shows, it was two standard devia-

Individual Tutoring Compared to Classroom Instruction

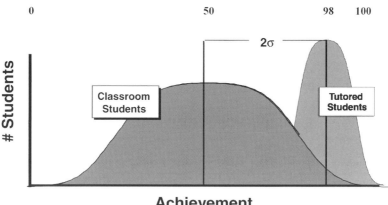

tions. This finding means, for example, that with instructional time held fairly constant one-on-one tutoring raised the performance of 50th percentile students to that of 98th percentile students. These, and similar empirical research findings, suggest that differences between one-on-one tutoring and typical classroom instruction are not only likely, but also very large.

Why then do we not provide these benefits to all students? The answer is straightforward and obvious. With the exception of a few critical skills, such as aircraft piloting and surgery, we cannot afford it. One-on-one tutoring has been described as an educational imperative and an economic impossibility.[4]

---

[3] Benjamin S. Bloom, "The 2 Sigma Problem: The Search for Methods of Group Instruction as Effective as One-to-One Tutoring." The dissertation studies were performed under Bloom's direction.

[4] M. Scriven, "Problems and Prospects for Individualization."

The success of one-on-one tutoring may be explained by two factors. First, measured in terms of questions asked and answered, tutors and their students engage in many more instructional interactions per unit of time than is possible in a classroom. Second, one-on-one tutoring can overcome the substantial spread of ability, measured by the time needed to reach minimal proficiency, that is found in practically every classroom. Tutoring reduces time-to-learn by adapting each interaction to the needs of each student. Less time is spent on material the student has already learned, and more time is spent on material remaining to be mastered.

To investigate the intensity of instructional interactions, Art Graesser and Natalie Person compared questioning and answering in classrooms with those in tutorial settings.[5] They found that classroom groups of students ask about three questions an hour and that any single student in a classroom asks about 0.11 questions per hour. In contrast, they found that students in individual tutorial sessions asked 20–30 questions an hour and were required to answer 117–146 questions per hour. Reviews of the intensity of interaction that occurs in technology-based instruction have found even more active student response levels.[6]

Differences in the time needed by individuals in any classroom to meet instructional objectives are also substantial. Studies on this issue have reported ratios varying from 1:3 to 1:7 in the times the fastest learners need to learn compared to the times needed by the slowest learners. Although these differences may be due initially to ability, these studies suggest that such ability is quickly overtaken by prior knowledge of the subject matter.[7] This effect is particularly evident in instruction for post-secondary-school students, because prior knowledge rapidly increases with age and experience. Technology-based instruction has long been recognized for its ability to adjust the pace of instruction to individual needs, advancing through instructional material as quickly or as slowly as required. The overall result has been substantial savings in the time required to meet given instructional objectives.[8]

It should be emphasized that these benefits are not achieved at the expense of instructional quality. Research has found that many instructional technologies have a positive impact on learning across a wide variety of student populations, settings, and instructional subject matters.[9]

This research suggests that technology-based instruction results in substantial savings of time and money. Studies have shown that the times saved aver-

---

[5] Art Graesser and Natalie Person, "Question-Asking During Tutoring."

[6] J. D. Fletcher, *Technology, the Columbus Effect, and the Third Revolution in Learning.*

[7] Sigmund Tobias, "When Do Instructional Methods Make a Difference?"

[8] J. D. Fletcher, "Evidence for Learning From Technology-Assisted Instruction."

[9] Ken Spencer, "Modes, Media and Methods: The Search for Educational Effectiveness."

age about 30 percent, as seen in the table below. The reduction in overhead expenses averages 20–30 percent.[10] Research has shown that the cost ratios (calculated as the ratio of experimental intervention costs over the costs of a control group) for interactive multimedia technology (computer-based instruction with enhanced audio, graphics, and/or video; CD-ROM and DVD-based instruction; interactive video, etc.) favor it over conventional instruction along with time savings of about 31 percent.[11] Simulation of such systems as helicopters, tanks, and command-control systems for training combat skills has also proven to be cost-effective.[12] The operational costs for simulation are, on average, 10 percent of the costs of using the actual systems to train.[13]

Time Savings for Technology-Based Instruction

Study (Reference)	Number of Studies Reviewed	Average Time Saved (Percent)
Military Training - Orlansky	13	54
Higher Education - Fletcher	8	31
Higher Education - Kulik	17	34
Adult Education - Kulik	15	24

Meta-analysis Demonstrates the Effectiveness of Instructional Technology

Researchers often use a meta-analytic approach to review and synthesize quantitative research studies on a variety of issues, including instructional effectiveness.[14] This method involves a three-step process, which begins with the collection of studies relevant to the issue using clearly defined procedures that can be replicated. Next, a quantitative measure, "effect size," is used to tabulate the outcomes of all the collected studies, including those with results that are not statistically significant. Finally, statistical procedures are used to

---

[10] Jesse Orlansky and Joseph String, *Cost-Effectiveness of Computer-Based Instruction in Military Training*; H. Solomon, *Economic Issues in Cost-Effectiveness Analyses of Military Skill Training*; James Kulik, "Meta-Analytic Studies of Findings on Computer-Based Instruction"; Rob Johnston, "The Effectiveness of Instructional Technology"; Ruth Phelps et al., "Effectiveness and Costs of Distance Education Using Computer-Mediated Communication"; J. D. Fletcher *Effectiveness and Cost of Interactive Videodisc Instruction in Defense Training and Education.*

[11] J. D. Fletcher, "Computer-Based Instruction: Costs and Effectiveness."

[12] Jesse Orlanksy et al., *The Cost and Effectiveness of the Multi-Service Distributed Training Testbed (MDT2) for Training Close Air Support.*

[13] Jesse Orlansky et al., *The Value of Simulation for Training.*

[14] Gene Glass, "Primary, Secondary, and Meta-Analysis of Research."

synthesize the quantitative measures and describe the findings of the analysis. Meta-analysis appears to be especially suited for synthesizing the results of instructional research, and it has been widely used for this purpose since its introduction in 1976.

Meta-analysis is still being developed as a technique, and some matters concerning its use, notably the "file-drawer" problem and calculation of effect size, remain unsettled. Chapter Twelve presents a more detailed explanation and these considerations. Briefly, however, meta-analytic reviews of instructional technology effectiveness have found substantial results favoring its use over traditional technologies of classroom instruction.

Overall, effect sizes for post-secondary school instruction average about 0.42, which is roughly equivalent to raising the achievement of 50th percentile students to that of 66th percentile students.[15] Reviews of more elaborate forms of instructional technology, such as those using applied artificial intelligent techniques, have found effect sizes in excess of 1.0, which is roughly equivalent to raising the achievement of 50th percentile students to that of the 84th percentile.[16] It seems reasonable to conclude that the reduced costs and reduced time to learn obtained in applications of instructional technology are not achieved at the expense of instructional effectiveness.

Encouraging as these favorable results are, our ability to apply instructional technology efficiently may be in its infancy. Findings thus far have been based on instructional applications intended to teach facts (e.g., What is the capital of Brazil? What is the Spanish word for chapel? Who was the first director of the Central Intelligence Agency?) concepts (e.g., What is a mass spectrometer used for? What is the difference between micro- and macro-economics? When must you use a torque wrench?), and procedures (e.g., How do you record a movie from television? How do you prepare a purchase requisition? How do you calibrate a radar repeater?). All intelligence analysts must possess a repertoire of facts, concepts, and procedures to perform their craft, and instructional technology holds great promise for increasing both the efficiency with which they might develop this repertoire and their access to instructional resources for doing so.

However, the capabilities analysts may seek through instruction are likely to include more abstract, or "higher," cognitive processes. For instance, in addition to learning a procedure, analysts may need the capability to recognize

---

[15] Chen-Lin Kulik., James Kulik and Barbara Shwalb, "Effectiveness of Computer-Based Adult Education: A Meta-Analysis"; Chen-Lin Kulik and James Kulik, "Effectiveness of Computer-Based Education in Colleges"; Rob Johnston and J. D. Fletcher, *A Meta-Analysis of the Effectiveness of Computer-Based Training for Military Instruction*; J. D. Fletcher, "Evidence for Learning from Technology-Assisted Instruction."

[16] Sherrie P. Gott, R. S. Kane, and Alan Lesgold , *Tutoring for Transfer of Technical Competence.*

the procedure's applicability in unfamiliar situations, modify it as needed, and use it to develop new approaches and procedures. Early on, Bloom discussed learning objectives as a hierarchy beginning with knowledge at the most rudimentary level and ascending through comprehension, application, analysis, and synthesis to evaluation.[17] Bloom's is not the only such hierarchy to emerge from research on instructional design, but it seems to be the best known, and it describes as well as any the various levels of knowledge, skill, and ability to which learners may aspire.

Current Research on Higher Cognitive Abilities

Analysts have begun to discuss development of the higher cognitive abilities needed to deal with unanticipated and novel challenges.[18] Components of such "cognitive readiness" may include:

- *Situation awareness*—the ability to comprehend the relevant aspects of a situation and use this understanding to choose reasonable courses of action.[19] Practice and feedback in complex, simulated environments have been shown to improve situation awareness.

- *Memory*—the ability to recall and/or recognize patterns in a situation that lead to likely solutions. It may be supported by two underlying theoretical mechanisms: *encoding specificity,*[20] which stresses the importance of responding to relevant external and internal perceptual cues, and *transfer-appropriate processing,*[21] which stresses the actions performed during encoding and retrieval. Some instructional techniques, such as overlearning,[22] have been shown to enhance long-term retention.[23]

- *Transfer*—the ability to apply what is learned in one context to a different context. It can be perceived either as the ability to select and apply procedural knowledge gained in one context to another ("low road" transfer) or as the ability to apply the principles abstracted from a set of contexts to another ("high road" transfer).[24] Extensive practice, with feedback, will

---

[17] Benjamin. S. Bloom, *Taxonomy of Educational Objectives.*

[18] J. E. Morrison, and J. D. Fletcher, *Cognitive Readiness.*

[19] M. R. Endsley, "Design and Evaluation for Situation Awareness Enhancement."

[20] E. Tulving and D. M. Thomson, "Encoding Specificity and Retrieval Processes in Episodic Memory."

[21] C. D. Morris, J. D. Bransford, and J. J. Franks, "Level of Processing Versus Transfer-Appropriate Processing."

[22] The use of specific problem-solving methods repetitively.

[23] R. A. Wisher, M. A. Sabol, and J. A. Ellis *Staying Sharp: Retention of Military Knowledge and Skills.*

enhance the former. Instruction in developing mental abstractions will enhance the latter.

- *Metacognition*—the executive functions of thought, more specifically, those needed to monitor, assess, and regulate one's own cognitive processes.[25] Meta-cognitive skills can be enhanced by exercises designed to increase awareness of self-regulatory processes.[26]

- *Pattern Recognition*—the ability to distinguish the familiar from the unfamiliar. It may be accomplished by "template matching," which involves comparing retained images with incoming sensory impressions; or by "feature comparison," which involves recognizing and generalizing from distinctive features of a structure held in memory with incoming sensory impressions.[27] Pattern recognition can be taught through a combination of extensive practice, with feedback, and instruction in forming abstractions.

- *Automaticity*—processes that require only limited conscious attention.[28] Automaticity can be taught by providing extensive practice, with feedback.

- *Problem Solving*—the ability to analyze a situation and identify a goal or goals that flow from it, identify tasks and subtasks leading to the goal, develop a plan to achieve them, and apply the resources needed to carry out the plan. Practice, with feedback, and overlearning can enhance problem-solving ability in many tasks. Techniques for problem solving can be successfully taught, as can the knowledge base needed to implement them.[29]

- *Decisionmaking*—a component of problem solving, but the emphasis in decisionmaking is on recognizing learned patterns, reviewing courses of action, assessing their impact, selecting one, and allocating resources to it.[30] Instruction in assessing courses of action has been shown to improve decisionmaking, but some aspects of successful decisionmaking are more likely to be inborn than trained.

- *Mental Flexibility and Creativity*—the ability to generate and modify courses of action rapidly in response to changing circumstances.[31] It

---

[24] G. Salomon and D. N. Perkins "Rocky Roads to Transfer: Rethinking Mechanisms of a Neglected Phenomenon."

[25] J. H. Flavell, "Metacognitive Aspects of Problem Solving."

[26] D. J. Hacker, *Metacognition: Definitions and Empirical Foundations* [On-line Report].

[27] M. H. Ashcraft, *Fundamentals of Cognition.*

[28] R. M. Shiffrin and W. Schneider, W. "Controlled and Automatic Human Information Processing: II. Perceptual Learning."

[29] J. R. Hayes, *The Complete Problem Solver.*

[30] P. Slovic, S. Lichtenstein, and B. Fischoff, "Decision-making."

[31] D. Klahr, & H. A. Simon, "What Have Psychologists (and Others) Discovered About the Process of Scientific Discovery?"

includes the ability to devise plans and actions that differ from and improve upon "school solutions." Capabilities that widen the range of options can be taught, but higher levels of creativity are more likely to be inborn than trained.

The above review suggests, first, that the creative processes needed by analysts can, to some extent, be broken down into components, and second, that these components can, again to some extent, be taught. Instructional technology can now substantially aid analysts in acquiring the facts, concepts, and procedures needed to perform their craft. However, it must become increasingly "intelligent" if it is to compress the years of experience analysts now need to become proficient and help them more rapidly acquire the advanced cognitive capabilities—those higher in Bloom's hierarchy—that they also need. To do this successfully, instruction must be tailored to the specific background, abilities, goals, and interests of the individual student or user. Instructional technology must provide what has been called "articulate expertise." Not only must it supply helpful and relevant guidance in these more advanced levels of knowledge, skills, and abilities, it must do so in a way that learners and users with varying levels of knowledge and skill can understand.

Discussion

At this point, it may be worth reviewing the capabilities provided by "non-intelligent" instructional technology since the 1950s. It has been able to:[32]

- accommodate the rate of progress of individual students, allowing as much or as little time as each needs to reach instructional objectives;

- tailor both the content and the sequence of instructional content to each student's needs;[33]

- make the instruction easy or difficult, specific or abstract, applied or theoretical as necessary;

- adjust to students' most efficient learning styles (collaborative or individual, verbal or visual, etc.).

Intelligent tutoring systems are a different matter. They require quite specific capabilities that were first targeted in the 1960s.[34] Two key capabilities are that intelligent tutoring systems must:

---

[32] E. Galanter, *Automatic Teaching*; R. C. Atkinson and H. A. Wilson, *Computer-Assisted Instruction*; P. Suppes and M. Morningstar, *Computer-assisted Instruction at Stanford 1966-68*; J. D. Fletcher and M. R. Rockway, "Computer-based Training in the Military."

[33] J. S. Brown, R. R. Burton, and J. DeKleer, "Pedagogical, Natural Language and Knowledge Engineering in SOPHIE I, II, and III."

- allow either the system or the student to ask open-ended questions and initiate instructional, "mixed-initiative" dialogue as needed or desired;

- generate instructional material and interactions on demand instead of requiring developers to foresee and store all the materials and interactions needed to meet all possible eventualities.

Mixed-initiative dialogue requires a language for information retrieval, tools to assist decisionmaking, and instruction that is shared by both the system and the student/user. The system must have the capability (referred to as "generative capability") to devise, on demand, interactions with students that do not rely on predicted and prestored formats. This capability involves more than generating problems tailored to each student's needs. It must also provide the interactions and presentations that simulate one-on-one tutorial instruction, including coaching, hints, and critiques of completed solutions.

Cost containment is one motivation for wanting to generate responses to all possible student states and actions instead of attempting to anticipate and store them. Another arises from basic research on human learning, memory, perception, and cognition. As documented by Neisser among others, during the 1960s and 1970s, the emphasis in basic research on human behavior and on the way in which it is understood shifted from the strict logical positivism of behavioral psychology, which focused on directly observable actions, to consideration of the internal, cognitive processes that were needed to explain empirically observed behavioral phenomena and are assumed to mediate and enable human learning.[35]

The hallmark of this approach is the view that seeing, hearing, and remembering are all acts of *construction,* making more or less use of the limited stimulus information provided by our perceptual capabilities. Constructivist approaches are the subject of much current and relevant discussion in instructional research circles, but they are firmly grounded in the foundations of scientific psychology.[36] For instance, in 1890, William James stated his General Law of Perception: "Whilst part of what we perceive comes through our senses from the object before us, another part (and it may be the larger part) always comes out of our mind."[37]

In this sense, the generative capability sought by intelligent instructional systems is not merely something nice to have. It is essential if we are to

---

[34] J. R. Carbonell, "AI in CAI: An Artificial Intelligence Approach to Computer-Assisted Instruction"; J. D. Fletcher & M. R. Rockway.

[35] U. Neisser, *Cognitive Psychology.*

[36] For example, T. M. Duffy, and D. H. Jonassen, *Constructivism and the Technology of Instruction*; S. Tobias and L. T. Frase, "Educational psychology and training."

[37] William James, *Principles of Psychology: Volume I.*

advance beyond the constraints of the prescribed, prebranched, programmed learning and ad hoc principles commonly used to design technology-based instruction. The long-term vision is that training, education, and performance improvement will take the form of human-computer conversations.

There has been progress toward this end. This conversational capability has been realized in systems that can discuss issues with students using a formal language, such as computer programming or propositional calculus.[38] More recent research suggests that significantly improved natural-language dialogue capabilities can be achieved by instructional technology.[39] Such an interactive, generative capability is needed if we are to deal successfully with the extent, variety, and mutability of human cognition. Much can now be accomplished by instructional technology, but much more can be expected.

Conclusion

The research discussed above suggests that instructional technology can:

- reduce costs of instruction;
- increase the accessibility of instruction;
- increase instructional effectiveness for analysts;
- reduce the time analysts need to learn facts, concepts, and procedures;
- track progress and ensure that all learners achieve instructional targets;
- provide opportunities for helping analysts to compress experience and achieve the higher cognitive levels of mastery demanded by their craft.

In addition, the findings suggest a rule of "thirds." This rule posits that the present state-of-the-art in instructional technologies can reduce the cost of instruction by about a third and *either* increase achievement by about a third *or* decrease time to reach instructional objectives by a third. Eventually, instructional technology should provide a conversation between the analyst and the technology that will tailor instruction in real time and on demand to the particular knowledge, skills, abilities, interests, goals, and needs of each individual. This capability, now available in rudimentary forms, can be expected to improve and develop with time. Even in its current state of development, however, instructional technology deserves serious attention within the Intelligence Community.

---

[38] For example, BIP and EXCHECK, respectively. For the first, see A. Barr, M. Beard, and R. C. Atkinson, "A rationale and description of a CAI Program to teach the BASIC Programming Language"; for the second, see P. Suppes and M. Morningstar.

[39] A. C. Graesser, M. A. Gernsbacher, and S. Goldman, *Handbook of Discourse Processes.*

CHAPTER EIGHT

Organizational Culture: Anticipatory Socialization and Intelligence Analysts

Stephen H. Konya[1]
Rob Johnston

I know it sounds silly, but I had this image of James Bond before I started working here. The truth is, I just sit in a cubicle, and I write reports.

Every organization has a unique culture that is defined partly by its individual members and partly by its structure, history, and policies. For that culture to endure, it must be transmitted from current members to new members. This process, known as organizational socialization, is especially important in organizations with strong, insular cultures, as those with weak cultures have less to transmit and will tend to experience culture changes as members come and go.

Although socialization begins prior to a person's first day on the job and is a continuous process, it is experienced most intensely by new employees. The cultural symbols acquired and interpreted during their initial interaction with the institution create potent and lasting impressions.[2] For them, socialization

---

[1] Stephen Konya is a Research Associate at the Institute for Defense Analyses, currently examining multimodal interfaces for the dismounted for the DARPA/Army Future Combat Systems program. He holds an MS in industrial and organizational psychology from Rensselaer Polytechnic Institute.

[2] Umberto Eco, *A Theory of Semiotics*; Clifford Geertz, *The Interpretation of Cultures*; Jacques Lacan, *Ecrits*; Ferdinand de Saussure, *Course in General Linguistics*.

is the process of learning the ropes; training; and becoming formally and informally acquainted with what is actually of value within the organization.[3] It is also the time when one learns the organization's norms and taboos and the extent of its social capital.[4] In sum, formal and informal socialization are types of control mechanism for maintaining the norms, or status quo, within any organization.[5]

Organizational Socialization

According to Daniel Feldman, organizational socialization is "the process through which individuals are transformed from outsiders to participating, effective members of an organization."[6] As shown in Figure 1, Feldman divides this process into three stages: getting in (or anticipatory socialization), breaking in (or accommodation), and settling in (often referred to as role management). During the getting-in stage, potential employees try to acquire information about an organization from available sources, such as Web sites, professional journals, and corporate annual reports. The breaking-in stage includes orientation and learning organizational as well as job-related proce-

Feldman's three stages of organizational socialization.

dures. The settling-in stage concludes when an individual attains full member status in the organization.

While each of the three stages of socialization is important, the focus of this chapter is on the first, or anticipatory, stage. There are several reasons for this. Clearly, the expectations people develop about an organization they are joining are important to a new recruit's eventual satisfaction, retention, and performance. Moreover, because it can control several aspects of the recruitment process, this stage is often the easiest for an organization to change. This chapter will take both a descriptive and prescriptive approach to easing the socialization of new employees.

---

[3] William G. Tierney and Robert A. Rhoads, *Faculty Socialization as Cultural Process.*
[4] See footnote 7 in Chapter Two.
[5] John P. Wanous, *Organizational Entry.*
[6] Daniel C. Feldman, "The Multiple Socialization of Organization Members."

Anticipatory Socialization

Anticipatory socialization encompasses all of the learning that occurs prior to a recruit's entering on duty.[7] At this stage, an individual forms expectations about the job and makes decisions about the suitability of fit between himself and the organization. What a person has heard about working for a particular organization, such as an intelligence agency, provides an idea of what to expect if hired. Conversely, individuals who do not believe they would fit in may decide not to apply.

There are two variables that are particularly useful for tracking a potential employee's progress through the anticipatory stage: The first is *realism*, or the extent to which an individual acquires an accurate picture of daily life in the organization. Realism is influenced by the level of success recruits achieve during the information-sharing and information-evaluation part of their recruitment. The second is *congruence*, or the extent to which the organization's resources and the individual's needs and skills are mutually satisfying. Congruence is influenced by the level of success an individual has achieved in making decisions about employment. Although it cannot directly influence congruence, which is an inherently personal experience, an organization can present relevant information in order to provide a realistic and accurate description of the work performed and the work environment.

Organizations often use interviews to begin the socialization of new recruits. For example, an interviewer will attempt to provide an accurate description of what to expect from the job and the organization, the purpose being to reduce the likelihood that a recruit will be disturbed by unanticipated situations. Interviewing is also used to determine the degree to which there is a match between the values of potential recruits and the values of the organization. New recruits with personal values matching those of the organization have been found to adjust to the organization's culture more quickly than recruits with nonmatching values.[8]

Organizations also send cultural messages to new recruits during interviews. When there are several rounds of interviews with progressively senior members of the organization, for example, the message conveyed is that finding the best person for the position is important. In contrast, hiring for a part-time job at the lowest level of the organization is often accomplished quickly, to the extent that a person having minimally acceptable qualifications may

---

[7] This stage is termed "pre-arrival" in Lyman W. Porter, Edward E. Lawler, and J. Richard Hackman, *Behavior in Organizations*.

[8] Jerald Greenberg and Robert A. Baron, *Behavior in Organizations*: *Understanding the Human Side of Work*.

often be hired on the spot. The cultural message in this case is that such employees are easily let in to and out of the organization.

Another, particularly pertinent example is intelligence work, which requires that recruits undergo employment screenings unlike those found in most civilian jobs. Potential CIA analysts must submit to a thorough background investigation, a polygraph examination, and financial and credit reviews. Further, a battery of psychological and medical exams must be passed prior to a formal employment offer. The timeframe for the background check eliminates the possibility of a rapid hiring decision. Even more important are the nonverbal messages sent to the recruit that this is a position of secrecy and high importance.

Several sources of information contribute to beliefs about any organization. Friends or relatives who are already part of the organization might share their experiences with the person considering employment. Information might also be acquired from other sources, such as professional journals, magazines, newspaper articles, television, governmental and private Web sites, public statements or testimony, and annual reports. While these sources of information about an organization are far from perfect (all may contain positive and negative hyperbole), they are still useful from the point of view of forming preliminary ideas about what it might be like to work for that organization.

Because competition for highly qualified employees is fierce, successful recruitment usually involves a skillful combination of salesmanship and diplomacy. Recruiters tend to describe their organizations in glowing terms, glossing over internal problems and external threats, while emphasizing positive features. The result is that potential employees often receive unrealistically positive impressions of conditions prevailing in a specific organization. When they arrive on the job and find that their expectations are not met, they experience disappointment, dissatisfaction, and even resentment that they have been misled. In fact, research findings indicate that the less employees' job expectations are met, the less satisfied and committed they are and the more likely they are to think about quitting or actually to do so.[9]

These negative reactions are sometimes termed entry shock, referring to the confusion and disorientation experienced by many newcomers to an organization. In order to avoid entry shock, it is important for organizations to provide job candidates with accurate information about the organization. Research supports the notion that people exposed to realistic job previews later report higher satisfaction and show lower turnover than those who receive glowing, but often misleading, information about their companies.[10] Moreover, having

---

[9] John P. Wanous et al., "The Effects of Met Expectations on Newcomer Attitudes and Behavior: A Review and Meta-analysis."

[10] Bruce M. Meglino et al., "Effects of Ralistic Job Previews: A Comparison Using an Enhancement and a Reduction Preview."

realistic expectations helps to ease the accommodation stage of the socialization process.

Consequences of Culture Mismatch

When I got here, I felt like a rabbit stuck in headlights. Now, I feel like a deer.

It took me a while to figure out that this place runs more like a newspaper than a university.

It's pretty solitary work. I spend all day in my head. I really wasn't expecting that.

There are several consequences of a cultural mismatch between an employee and an organization. Among these consequences are culture shock, low job satisfaction, low employee morale, increased absenteeism, increased turnover, and increased costs.

Culture Shock. People often have to be confronted with different cultures before they become conscious of their own culture. In fact, when people are faced with new cultures, it is not unusual for them to become confused and disoriented, a phenomenon commonly referred to as culture shock.

Beryl Hesketh and Stephen Bochner, among others, have observed that the process of adjusting to another culture generally follows a U-shaped curve.[11] At first, people are optimistic about learning a new culture. This excitement is followed by frustration and confusion as they struggle to learn the new culture. After six months or so with the organization, people adjust to their new cultures, become more accepting of them, and are more satisfied by them. For those who enter a mismatched culture, the productivity issue is clear: the several months required to adjust and accept the new work style results in several months of even lower productivity than is obtainable with those who fit in right away.

Job Satisfaction. Job satisfaction is defined by one scholar as "people's positive or negative feelings about their jobs."[12] It is hardly surprising that dissatisfied employees may try to find ways of reducing their exposure to their jobs. This is especially significant when one considers that people spend roughly one-third of their lives at work.

---

[11] Beryl Hesketh and Stephen Bochner, "Technological Change in a Multicultural Context: Implications for Training and Career Planning"; Maddy Janssens, "Interculture Interaction: A Burden on International Managers?"
[12] Edwin A. Locke, "The Nature and Causes of Job Satisfaction."

Interestingly, research suggests that the relationship between satisfaction and task performance, although positive, is not especially strong.[13] Thus, while job satisfaction may be important to the longevity of any individual career cycle, it is not a major factor in individual job performance. It does, however, increase absenteeism, which has a negative effect on overall organizational productivity.

Absenteeism and Turnover. Research indicates that the lower an individual's job satisfaction, the more likely he or she is to be absent from work.[14] As with job satisfaction and task performance, this relationship is modest but also statistically significant. An employee may even choose to leave an organization altogether. This voluntary resignation is measured as employee turnover and has fiscal consequences for both the individual and the organization.

Fiscal Cost. Employee turnover is a critical cost element. The expense of recruiting and training new employees, along with lost productivity from vacant positions and overtime pay for replacement workers, increases operating costs and also reduces employee organizational output.

A 2002 study by the Employment Policy Foundation found that the estimated turnover cost is $12,506 per year per full-time vacancy for the average employee with total compensation (wages and benefits) of $50,025.[15] As the average annual turnover benchmark within the Fortune 500 is 23.8 percent, one can clearly see how critical it is for organizations to lessen the number of employees who leave voluntarily. Even unscheduled absences can be expensive—averaging between $247 and $534 per employee, per day, according to the same study.

Anticipatory Socialization in the Intelligence Community

The secrecy is strange. I thought it would be romantic, but it turns out that it is just strange.

I was sold on the cool factor. It's still sort of cool, I guess.

Accepting a job with one of the 14 members of the Intelligence Community differs from other professions in that it is difficult for new employees to have a clear and precise understanding of the roles and responsibilities they are about

---

[13] The correlation is 0.17 according to Michelle T. Iaffaldano and Paul M. Muchinsky in their "Job Satisfaction and Job Performance: A Meta-Analysis."

[14] Lyman W. Porter et al., "Organizational Commitment, Job Satisfaction and Turnover Among Psychiatric Technicians."

[15] This number does not take into account the additional costs within the Intelligence Community for background and security investigations.

to assume. This is all the more pronounced because, for the most part, the Intelligence Community organizations lack a civilian counterpart.

Occasionally, the anticipatory socialization of people entering the intelligence analysis discipline will derive from accounts of current or former practitioners. More generally, however, a newcomer's initial impressions stem from the fictional media portrayals, which tend to emphasize the supposed glamour of operational tasks and pay little attention to the reality of research-based analytic work. The absence of hard knowledge about intelligence work is attributable, in part, to the organizational secrecy of the Intelligence Community and, in part, to the actual socialization process that occurs after one has been accepted for employment and has passed the required background investigation.

A newcomer's experience is often contrary to initial expectations. Employees are discouraged from talking about the specifics of their work outside of the organization or with those who have not been "cleared." On an individual level, this experience translates into professional culture shock and social isolation. Organizationally, an intentionally closed system of this kind has a number of potential performance-related consequences, among them perpetuation of the existing organizational culture by hiring familial legacies or those most likely to "fit in," job dissatisfaction, low morale and consequent reduction in employee readiness, increased employee turnover, greater likelihood of "groupthink," and strong internal resistance to organizational change.[16]

Since the attacks of 11 September, the Intelligence Community has become more open about its role in government, its day-to-day working environment, and its employees' functions and responsibilities. While this openness is an extension of an ongoing trend toward public outreach—an example is the CIA's Officer-in-Residence program established in 1985—the community has accelerated this trend toward openness in an effort to help the public, and its representatives, understand the missions and value of the Intelligence Community.[17]

This trend toward openness has improved employee retention by counteracting the culture shock of misinformed anticipatory socialization and resultant employee turnover. This trend also helps prepare the organization for the inevitable changes to come by increasing the potential recruitment pool, expanding the intellectual diversity of its staff, and fostering better relations with its broader constituency, the American public.

---

[16] Irving Janis, *Groupthink*.
[17] See CIA Officer in Residence Program in Web Resources in bibliography.

Conclusion and Recommendations

As noted, there is something of a disconnect between the largely fictionalized portrayal of the Intelligence Community in the popular media and the actual experience of intelligence analysts. This disconnect can be exacerbated once a recruit is on the job and can lead to negative consequences and behaviors, such as organizational culture shock, employee dissatisfaction, and increased employee absenteeism and turnover. This has an obvious effect on individual analysts, but it has a direct effect on the efficiency and effectiveness of the Intelligence Community.

Since the September 2001 attacks, some members of the Intelligence Community have acted to change the socialization process by providing accurate and realistic career information. One of the most widely used media for this is the Internet. For example, the Central Intelligence Agency's (CIA) Web site contains a section on "Life at the CIA."[18] This section contains information about the Agency and its culture, several analyst profiles and job descriptions written in the analyst's own words, and information concerning employee benefits and social and intellectual diversity. Although the "Employment" section of the Federal Bureau of Investigation's (FBI) Web site is less detailed than the "Life at the CIA" section of the CIA Web site, it does illustrate a typical first assignment.[19] In contrast, the "Careers" section of the Defense Intelligence Agency's (DIA) Web site contains detailed information on current job openings and the application process, but it provides no information about the actual work of a DIA analyst.[20] Steps such as these are encouraging, but they are still insufficient. There are more active things that can be done to facilitate the socialization of new employees.

To begin, Intelligence Community components should accept that what most people know about a job is often false and that it is incumbent on the organization and its recruiters to present accurate pictures and to work diligently to dispel myths. This will help to counteract the effects of culture shock. Instead of overselling a particular job or organization, recruiters should focus on facilitating the anticipatory socialization of potential employees by providing accurate information about the job and about the culture of the organization itself. Early in the selection process, applicants should be provided with realistic job previews, presented in either written or oral form. Previews should contain accurate information about the specific conditions within an organization and the specific requirements of the job. Research has shown that providing accurate descriptions of tasks is important in increasing job commitment and job satisfaction, as well as decreasing initial turnover of new

---

[18] See Central Intelligence Agency Web site in Web Resources.
[19] See Federal Bureau of Investigation Web site in Web Resources
[20] See Defense Intelligence Agency and US Intelligence Community Web sites in Web Resources.

employees.[21] The job preview allows candidates to make an informed decision to continue with the recruitment process or to withdraw from it if they feel the job is not appropriate. Realistic previews also lower unrealistically high expectations. A particularly good example of such an effort can be found on the CIA's Office of General Counsel Web site. This Web site includes a section titled "Misconceptions about working for the CIA," which tries to dispel prejudices and biases about employment at the CIA by addressing them in a straightforward manner.[22] In addition, the authors explain the benefits of having work experiences with the CIA for future employment endeavors in other areas.

Interview screenings of applicants should be reviewed and improved where needed. Hiring interviews are not very effective predictors of job performance; even so, there are ways to improve their reliability and validity. Numerous cognitive measurement instruments are available that help predict a match between an individual's knowledge, skills, and abilities and specific behavioral, cognitive, and psychomotor tasks.[23] In addition, the use of structured interviewing - posing the same questions to all applicants - is more effective than unstructured interviewing. Structured interviews allow for consistent comparisons among applicants.[24] Organizations should also consider using panel interviews. Differences among individual interviewers may result in inaccurate judgment of an applicant, but the overall decision of a team of evaluators may improve reliability.[25]

The use of situational exercises should be included in the recruitment process. These exercises usually consist of approximations of specific aspects of a job. They can be used to evaluate candidates' job abilities and to provide candidates with simulated work tasks. The former can facilitate organizational evaluations of candidates' performance on a job-related task; the latter may help candidates to decide whether the job would be a good match.[26]

A desirable additional step would be the creation and expansion of academic degree programs with a focus on intelligence and intelligence analysis. Further, an enhanced effort to improve public awareness and understanding of the Intelligence Community through greater community outreach, internships,

---

[21] Glenn M. McEvoy and Wayne F. Cascio, "Strategies for Reducing Employee Turnover: A Meta-analysis."

[22] See Central Intelligence Agency, Office of General Counsel Web site.

[23] The Buros Institute of Mental Measurements tracks and reports the statistical validity and reliability of thousands of measurement instruments.

[24] Richard D. Arvey and James E. Campion, "The Employment Interview: A Summary of Recent Research."

[25] P. L. Roth and James E. Campion, "An Analysis of the Predictive Power of the Panel Interview and Pre-Employment Tests."

[26] Wayne F. Cascio, *Applied Psychology in Human Resource Management.*

research fellowships, professional workshops, and academic forums will help to facilitate better employee relations by providing potential employees with a clearer perspective on what to expect after receiving their badge.

CHAPTER NINE
Recommendations

The First Step: Recognizing A Fundamental Problem

It is far too early in the research process to determine if any one organizational model for the Intelligence Community is more or less effective than any other, but I believe there is a fundamental structural question that needs to be addressed at the outset. This is, in my view, that current reporting competes for time and resources with indications and warning (I&W) intelligence. This emphasis is unlikely to change, for several reasons. First, current intelligence reporting results in significant "face-time" for the Intelligence Community with policy makers, who, in turn, provide the resources that fund and support community activities. This is a significant contributor to the social capital that the Intelligence Community commands.

The second reason is that in-depth research of the kind that contributes to I&W intelligence is a long-term investment whose payoff is often an abstraction. Not infrequently, successful warnings are taken for granted. Those that fail, however, may well involve the community in public recriminations that cost the Intelligence Community significant social capital. In this sense, the Intelligence Community's focus on current reporting is understandable. The problem is that producing current intelligence tends to become an all-consuming activity. The majority of analysts who participated in this study said that their time was spent on current reporting. Unfortunately, this does little to improve I&W intelligence, which requires long-term research, in-depth expertise, adoption of scientific methods, and continuous performance improvement. The return for the Intelligence Community, in terms of social capital, may be quite limited and even, as noted above, negative. Thus, the analytic area most in need of long-term investment often gets the least.

As the resources available to intelligence analysis are limited, it needs to be determined if those resources are better spent on the reporting functions of the Intelligence Community or on warning functions. It also needs to be determined whether these functions should be performed by the same analysts or if they are two separate career tracks. To make this determination, the Intelligence Community will need to invest in what I call a Performance Improvement Infrastructure as well as basic and applied analytic research.

Performance Improvement Infrastructure

The first step in improving job or task-specific performance is the establishment of a formal infrastructure designed explicitly to create an iterative performance improvement process. Such a process would include:

- measuring actual analytic performance to create baseline data;
- determining ideal analytic performance and standards;
- comparing actual performance with ideal performance;
- identifying performance gaps;
- creating interventions to improve analytic performance;
- measuring actual analytic performance to evaluate the effectiveness of interventions.

Several organizational, or infrastructure, assets should be developed to support this process. These should include:

- basic and applied research programs;
- knowledge repositories;
- communities of practice;
- development of performance improvement techniques.

The performance improvement process would be repeated throughout the life cycle of an organization in order to encourage continuous improvement. With the infrastructure and process in place, an organization would be capable of adapting to new or changing environmental conditions.

Infrastructure Requirements

Institutional changes, such as corporate reorganizations, are often enacted without a clear understanding of their potential or actual impact. What is most often missing in such changes is a basic research plan or a systems approach to determine and predict the effect on organizational performance. The same is true with the Intelligence Community. Although there have been numerous proposals to reorganize the Intelligence Community—including those that resulted from the hearings of the Kean 9/11 commission—few have addressed the question of why one change would be any more effective than any other change. Merely asserting, based on some a priori notion of effectiveness, that organizational scheme X is more effective than organizational scheme Y is insufficient evidence. What is needed is a posteriori data, such as case studies, to support or refute the proposed change.[1]

Organizational Requirements. Many large organizations distribute performance improvement responsibilities throughout the organization at a supervisory or midlevel of management, but the group most often charged with collecting and analyzing performance data is the human resources department. This task generally involves developing task-specific performance standards and metrics based on expert performance models and in accordance with corporate policy.

The human resources department also becomes the central repository for pre-, periodic, and post-performance measurements. As this department generally has contact with employees throughout their careers, this is the most efficient way to manage, analyze, and inform senior leadership about aggregate changes in performance over time. Although data are collected at the individual level, it is the aggregation of performance data that allows leadership to determine the effectiveness of any organizational change or job-related intervention.

Baseline Data. Measuring actual analytic performance is essential to the establishment of a data driven performance infrastructure. The analysts in this study perceived their performance to be tied directly to the quantity of written products they produced during each review period. Counting the number of analytic publications is one metric, of course, but it is hardly indicative of analytic quality. Surgeons are a useful example of this problem.. They may count the number of patients they treat, but this metric says more about system throughput and salesmanship than it does about surgical performance. Unlike the purely cognitive work of intelligence analysts, surgeons have the advantage of multiple physical outputs, which makes measurement an easier task. In particular, surgeons have patient outcomes, or morbidity and mortality ratios, which become a grounded end-state for all measurements.[2] Other things being equal, these data then ought to inform a prospective patient about where to take his or her business.

---

[1] William Nolte, a deputy assistant director of central intelligence for analysis and production proposed such an idea in "Preserving Central Intelligence: Assessment and Evaluation in Support of the DCI " in *Studies in Intelligence* 48, no. 3 (2004): 21–25.

For intelligence analysts, the question may be put as, "What is an analytic morbidity and mortality ratio?" The process of describing and identifying morbidity and mortality, or error and failure in analytical terms, is a necessary step in identifying mechanisms to develop, test, and implement performance improvement interventions. There was little consensus among the participants in this study about what comprises failure, or even if failure was possible. There was greater consensus regarding the nature of analytic error, which was generally thought to be a consequence of analytic inaccuracy.

Metrics. One could reasonably conclude that compounded errors lead to analytic failure. Conversely, one could conclude that failure is the result of analytic surprise, that its causes are different from the causes of error, and that it needs to be treated as a separate measurement. This subject is open to debate and will require further research. It is still possible, however, to use both accuracy and surprise as metrics in evaluating analytic performance on a case-by-case basis.

The advantage of an error and failure metric is that it is observable in a grounded state separate from the analytic process. Any analytic product can be reviewed to determine levels of accuracy, and any unexpected event can be traced back through analytic products to determine if there was an instance of surprise.

Once levels of error and failure are calculated, along with measures of output, it is possible to determine expert levels of performance and to derive performance models based on successful processes. In any organization, there will be those individuals with the greatest output—in this case, the greatest number of written products. There will also be individuals with the highest levels of accuracy—in this case, factual consistency. There will also be individuals who have the lowest incident of surprise—in this case, those who generate the greatest number of potential scenarios and track and report probabilities most reliably. Using data-driven metrics means that expertise is not a function of tenure; rather, it is a function of performance.

Once expert performers are identified, it is possible to capture their work processes and to develop performance models based on peak efficiency and effectiveness within the Intelligence Community. Through the use of cognitive, behavioral, and linguistic task analyses, ethnography, and controlled experiments, it is possible to generate process metrics to identify analytic methods that are more effective for specific tasks than other methods. This is not to say that there is one analytic method that is the most effective for intel-

---

[2] Grounded Theory is the development of theoretical constructs that result from performing interpretive analysis on qualitative data rather than relying on a priori insights. The theory is then derived from some grounded data set. Barney Glaser and Anselm Strauss, *Discovery of Grounded Theory*; Barney Glaser, *Theoretical Sensitivity*; Barney Glaser, *Basics of Grounded Theory Analysis*.

ligence analysis; rather, each type of task will have an analytic method that is best suited to accomplishing it in an efficient and effective manner.

Developing these metrics is no small task. It is a job that will require numerous researchers and research programs within, or with access to, the Intelligence Community. These programs will need formal relationships with human resource departments, analytic divisions, organizational leadership, and developers of training and technology interventions in order to have a positive effect on analytic performance.

Research Programs

The results of this research indicate that the Intelligence Community needs to commit itself to performance research that is rigorous, valid (in that it measures what it proposes to measure), and replicable (in that the method is sufficiently transparent that anyone can repeat it). Within some intelligence organizations, this has been an ongoing process. The problem is that most of the internal research has concentrated on historical case studies and the development of technological innovations. What is missing is focused study of human performance within the analytic components of the Intelligence Community. Questions about the psychology and basic cognitive aptitude of intelligence analysts, the effectiveness of any analytic method, the effectiveness of training interventions, group processes versus individual processes, environmental conditions, and cultural-organizational effects need to be addressed.

This effort will require commitment. Researchers will have to be brought into the Intelligence Community, facilities will have to be dedicated to researching analytic performance, expert analysts will have to give some percentage of their time to participating in research studies, managers and supervisors will have to dedicate time and resources to tracking analytic performance within their departments, human resource staffs will have to dedicate time and resources to developing a performance repository, and there will have to be formal interaction between researchers and the community.

Analytic Performance Research. In the previous section, I discussed the need for analytic standards as part of the Performance Improvement Infrastructure. In terms of a research program, this will require, as a first step, the collection of baseline analytic performance data and a clear and measurable description of ideal analytic behavior. Next, there should be a determined effort by human performance researchers to develop, test, and validate analytic performance metrics and measurement systems. This will be a lengthy process. The accuracy and surprise measures suggested in this text require large historical and comparative data sets and are cumbersome and time consuming to perform. Conducting behavioral, cognitive, and linguistic task analyses requires significant research expertise, ample time, and broad organizational access.

In time, analytic performance research will become a highly specialized domain and will require continuous organizational access not normally available to outsiders. It will become necessary for the Intelligence Community to establish internal or cooperative research centers in order to acquire the research expertise necessary to analyze and effect performance improvement. There are numerous community outreach efforts on which these centers can be built. Those efforts need to be expanded, however, and those programs need to include domains beyond the traditional relationship between the Intelligence Community and political or geographic area experts.[3]

Institutional Memory. The results of this research program indicate that there is a loss of corporate knowledge in the Intelligence Community due to employee attrition and the lack of a central knowledge repository for capturing "lessons learned." A number of industries and government organizations, including the Departments of Defense and Energy and the National Aeronautics and Space Administration, already maintain centers for lessons learned as an information hub for its employees.[4]

These centers act as information repositories for successful and unsuccessful operations and interventions. Their purpose is to reduce the amount of organizational redundancy and levels of error and failure by tracking, analyzing, and reporting on after-action reviews and analytic outcome data.[5] The other primary function of these repositories is to establish networks for communities of practice within and among organizations.

Networked communities of practice allow professionals to interact, exchange methodological information, post and respond to individual case studies, and develop ad hoc teams of experts for specific problem solving tasks. With simple search tools, basic database software, and a simple network visualization interface, any analyst in the Intelligence Community would be able to identify any other expert whose domain specialty was needed to answer a specific question or solve a specific problem. Another advantage of this model is the development of formal and informal mentoring within the network. Any novice would be able to find an expert within the Intelligence Community and establish a relationship that would be beneficial to both. With appropriate incentives, experts would be encouraged to contribute to the network and make available their time and expertise for the purpose of mentoring.

---

[3] An example of researching the validity and reliability of metrics can be found in the *Buros Mental Measurement Yearbook* at the Buros Institute of Mental Measurements Web site.

[4] See the US Army Center for Army Lessons Learned (CALL) Web site, which has links to numerous other repositories.

[5] See Chapter Six for a more detailed explanation of the After Action Review process.

Intelligence analysis, like other fields of science, is a cognitive process. Although tools and technologies may be available to assist cognitive processes, such as measurement devices for physical scientists, technology is ultimately merely a tool to be designed and developed using a human-centered approach. As such, any new technology needs to be a passive tool, employed by analysts to solve specific problems or answer specific questions, rather than a restrictive reinterpretation of cognition according to the rules of binary computation and artificial intelligence theorists.[6]

Analytic Psychology and Cognition. As evidenced by the work of Richards Heuer and others, there is significant research to be conducted into the cognitive mechanisms involved in intelligence analysis.[7] Understanding and defining the heuristics used in performing intelligence analysis, as well as cognitive-load thresholds, multitasking requirements, mechanisms that generate cognitive biases, and the utilization of pattern recognition strategies and anomaly detection methods are all areas that will prove fundamental to improving analytic performance.

In addition to researching basic cognitive functions and intelligence analysis, this area of research will be valuable for understanding how external variables, such as time constraints and analytic production methods, affect the cognitive processing of individual analysts. Another result will be the development of future employee screening and selection tools that will match the specific cognitive requirements of intelligence analysis with each applicant's individual knowledge, skills, and abilities.

Analysts employ cognitive strategies that are time efficient in order to cope with the demands of producing daily written products, but such strategies are not necessarily the most effective analytic methods for increasing analytic accuracy and decreasing the occurrence of analytic surprise. In fact, improving analytic accuracy and avoiding surprise may require mutually exclusive analytic strategies. This line of inquiry will require baseline performance data generated through the development of performance metrics and conducted in conjunction with research in analytic methodology effectiveness. The results would then be integrated into a knowledge repository.

These types of studies will require experimental psychologists and cognitive scientists working in controlled laboratory environments with consistent access to working professional analysts.

---

[6] See Chapter Five for a more detailed description of the limitations of technological solutions.

[7] Richards J. Heuer, Jr., *Psychology of Intelligence Analysis*; William Brei, *Getting Intelligence Right*; Isaac Ben-Israel, "Philosophy and Methodology of Intelligence: The Logic of Estimate Process"; Klaus Knorr, *Foreign Intelligence and the Social Sciences*; Abraham Ben-Zvi, "The Study of Surprise Attacks." See also Marjorie Cline, Carla Christiansen and Judith Fontaine, *Scholar's Guide to Intelligence Literature*.

Development and Validation of Analytic Methods. The Intelligence Community routinely generates ad hoc methodologies to solve specific analytic problems or crises. However, once the problem has been solved, or the crisis averted, the new analytic method may or may not become part of the institutional memory. Often these new methods are lost and need to be re-created to address the next problem or crisis. In addition, these methods are seldom tested against other competing analytic methods for validity or reliability. It is difficult for an analyst to know which analytic method to employ in a given situation or requirement.

There are obvious inefficiencies in the current model. First, there is the loss of corporate knowledge each time an innovative analytic method is generated and subsequently abandoned. Second, there is no effectiveness testing center where analytic methods can be compared for specific cases. Although there are hundreds of analytic strategies, there is no way to determine which strategy is the most effective for any particular problem set.

The lack of an analytic methodology research agenda leads analysts to choose methods with which they are most familiar or to choose those dictated by circumstance, such as deadlines. Moreover, instead of advancing the concept that intelligence analysis is science and needs to be engaged in like any other scientific discipline, the paucity of effectiveness data supports a deep-seated community bias that analytic methods are idiosyncratic and, therefore, akin to craft.

The development of a research agenda for analytic methodology that is focused on collecting effectiveness and validation data is the first step in moving intelligence analysis from a tradecraft model to a scientific model. This may be the most culturally difficult recommendation to implement: there is cultural resistance to adopting a science-based model of intelligence analysis that is rooted in the traditions, norms, and values of the Intelligence Community. Another difficult step will be to introduce effectiveness data and corresponding analytic methods to the community at large and to incorporate these in future training programs.

Training Effectiveness. Successful analysis demands group cohesion and the implementation of consistent, effective analytic methods within the Intelligence Community. The best way to achieve this is through formal basic and advanced training programs. As noted earlier, several agencies within the community have invested resources in formal training programs, but these programs are unique to each agency and are often missing evaluations of student performance. Although most formal courses include a written subjective evaluation of the instructor, as well as the student's perception of the value of the course, the evaluation of student performance has yet to be formalized.

Without evaluating preintervention, or precourse, performance and following that with a postintervention evaluation, it is difficult to determine the effect that any training intervention will have on employee performance. In addition to formal measurements based on course objectives, it is important to collect performance data from managers and supervisors to evaluate the retention of training and the impact that training has had on actual day-to-day performance.

Developing performance metrics will inform and advance the training interventions currently employed in the Intelligence Community and will determine the gap between ideal performance and actual performance. As such, the system is an iterative process of setting performance standards, measuring actual performance, designing training interventions to improve performance, and evaluating the effects of those interventions on actual performance. The data derived from these interventions and measurements will then contribute to the growth of the knowledge repository and strengthen the ties created through the communities of practice.

Organizational Culture and Effectiveness. Identifying existing organizational norms and taboos is the first step to creating an internal dialogue about the future of an organization and its place in a competitive environment. Culture drives the operations of an organization, determines the people who are hired, enculturates new employees, establishes standards of behavior and systems of rewards, shapes an organization's products, and determines the social capital that any organization may possess. In short, culture defines an organization's identity to itself and to others.

Understanding the culture of the Intelligence Community and analyzing the effects of any performance intervention on that culture contributes to the evaluation of intervention effectiveness. Effective performance interventions will have a positive effect on the organization's culture and become themselves measurement instruments.

Developing cultural markers to track organizational change and performance improvement requires baseline ethnographic data and the identification of key cultural indicators. Once identified, cultural indicators such as language use, norms, and taboos would be measured at regular intervals and would serve as grounded data to determine levels of change within the organization. This would permit interventions to be modified before they became ritualized within the Intelligence Community.

The Importance of Access

The improvement of human performance often requires an organization to change its culture, and organizational leaders seldom possess sufficient power to mandate cultural change by edict. At best, management can introduce agents or agencies of change and manage their organization's culture in the same way they manage physical and financial resources. An organization's culture shapes individual behavior by establishing norms and taboos and, ultimately, determines the quality and character of an organization's products. Culture and product are inseparable, and one cannot be changed without affecting the other. The choice confronting any organization is to manage its institutional culture or to be managed by it.

There is no single path to carrying out the research recommended in this work. It could be performed at a single center or coordinated through several specific centers; it could be purely internal to the Intelligence Community; a cooperative effort among the community, academe, and national laboratories; or some combination of these. What is most important to effective implementation is that there be regular and open access among researchers and the Intelligence Community. This may appear simple enough, but access equals trust, and trust is difficult to establish in any domain. This is especially the case within the Intelligence Community. The Intelligence Community needs to increase its commitment to community outreach efforts. This study is one such effort.

During the course of my research, the value of access and the premium the community places on trust quickly became evident. At agency after agency, physical access restrictions, security clearances, forms, interviews, phone calls, questions, vetting, and more vetting were all signs of the value, not of secrecy per se, but of trust and access. Without this sort of cooperation, this research would have been impossible, and this is an important lesson that ought to inform future research programs.

PART IV

Notes on Methodology

CHAPTER TEN
Survey Methodology

This study included 489 interviews with intelligence professionals, academics, and researchers throughout the Intelligence Community. It also involved participation in intelligence training programs, workshops, and focus groups; direct observation of intelligence analysts performing their duties, and participant observation in a variety of analytic tasks. My access was not restricted to specific people, locations, or organizations. I was allowed to observe, interview, and participate in whatever manner I thought would be most beneficial to the research project.

Unlike other academic studies of the intelligence discipline (case studies or topic-specific postmortems, for example), this study was process oriented. It also differed from the work of Sherman Kent, Richards Heuer, and other intelligence professionals concerned with the process of intelligence analysis.[1] Rather than having an intelligence professional looking *out* to the social and behavioral sciences, this study had a social scientist looking *in* at the intelligence profession. Although some of the conclusions of this work may be similar to previous studies, the change in perspective has also led to some different findings.

It is important to keep in mind that cultural anthropology is a qualitative discipline and that, in general, its findings are descriptive and explanatory rather than inferential or predictive. The use of ethnographic methods to describe a culture, the environment in which that culture operates, and the work processes that culture has adopted is designed to generate testable theory that can be investigated experimentally or quasi-experimentally using other

---

[1] Sherman Kent, *Strategic Intelligence for American World Policy;* Richards J. Heuer, Jr., *Psychology of Intelligence Analysis.*

research methodologies. Additionally, ethnography is used to identify and describe the influence of different variables on cultural phenomena, again with a focus on developing testable theory. Unlike more quantitative disciplines, cultural anthropology is not traditionally employed experimentally to test theory or to generate predictive measures of statistical significance.

The findings in this work describe the data collected during this study, but they do not indicate the weight or general statistical effect of any one variable as opposed to any other variable. Although a single variable might have more effect on the error or failure rate of intelligence analysis, further quantitative research will be needed to determine those statistical values. Without additional quantitative support, it may not be possible to generalize from these findings.

Methodology

This study used an applied anthropological methodology for the collection and analysis of qualitative data.[2] A traditional approach to ethnography, the descriptive documentation of living cultures, was modified for use in post-industrial organizational settings.[3] This method included conducting interviews, directly observing analysts performing their jobs, participating in analytic tasks and training, and conducting focus groups. The settings for this research included the 14 members of the Intelligence Community, related government agencies, universities, think tanks, national laboratories, the National Archives and related presidential libraries, and private and corporate locations.

The background data were collected using a Q-sort literature review method, which is discussed in more detail in Chapters Three and Eleven. This procedure was followed by semi-structured interviews, direct observation, participant observation, and focus groups. The Q-sort method was employed specifically because of its utility for developing taxonomic categories.[4]

The identity of the research participants will not be revealed. Participant responses and observational data gathered during the research process have been tabulated and made anonymous or aggregated according to context and

---

[2] Erve Chambers, *Applied Anthropology: A Practical Guide;* Alexander Ervin, *Applied Anthropology*: *Tools and Perspectives for Contemporary Practice.*

[3] Russell Bernard, *Research Methods in Anthropology: Qualitative and Quantitative Approaches;* Robert Bogdan, *Participant Observation in Organizational Settings;* Norman Denzin and Yvonna Lincoln, *Handbook of Qualitative Research*; Jean Schensul and Margaret LeCompte, *Ethnographer's Toolkit. Vol. I - Vol. VII;* James Spradley, *Participant Observation;* Robert Yin, *Case Study Research: Design and Methods.*

[4] William Stephenson, *The Study of Behavior: Q-Technique and its Methodology.*

content and, thus, are not attributable to any specific individual. This is not simply the result of security procedures within the Intelligence Community; it is also the professional obligation of every member of the American Anthropological Association, as stated in the American Anthropological Association Code of Ethics.[5]

The interview technique employed in this study was semi-structured. Several specific questions about the participant's perception of the nature of intelligence, the analytic process, the intelligence production cycle, and intelligence errors and failures were standard throughout the interviews. Other questions, specific to the individual's job responsibilities, were tailored to each respondent. This method allowed for a more open-ended approach, which surveys and highly structured interviews do not. The semi-structured method is more akin to an open conversation (with consistent data collection constructs and probing questions) than to a formal interview, which helps put the respondents at ease and makes the entire process seem somewhat less contrived.

Access to interview participants was made possible through the Center for the Study of Intelligence. Individuals at CSI introduced me to their contacts throughout the Intelligence Community, including active and retired senior analysts, managers and senior leadership, as well as to academics and researchers. The various intelligence-training centers put me in touch with new hires and novice analysts. Each interviewee was asked to make recommendations and provide contact information for others who might be interested in participating in this research project. In addition, numerous interviewees were approached without a formal or informal introduction from a previous participant. Only four of the 489 individuals contacted to date have declined to participate in this study. This constitutes a participation rate of greater than 99 percent, which is unusually high for this type of research. Although a participation rate this high may be an artifact of the sampling method or of an organizational pressure to participate, it also may indicate a general desire within the Intelligence Community to support performance improvement research.

Unlike random sampling, purposive sampling is an attempt to collect data from specific data sources. In anthropological studies, purposive sampling is regularly used to address specific issues and to answer specific questions. Normally, this approach requires finding a "key informant" or someone on the inside of a specific culture who will become the researcher's ally and access agent. In this particular study, the CSI staff acted as access agents to the Intelligence Community at large.

---

[5] American Anthropological Association, *Code of Ethics of the American Anthropological Association.*

Relying on such a "social network" sampling method for collecting interview data does pose potential statistical biases.[6] The likelihood that each new interviewee was referred to me because of a friendly relationship with a previous interviewee may mean that those references are "like minded" and not necessarily representative of the population of intelligence professionals. In order to counteract that bias, efforts were also made to enlist individuals without any social network-based introduction. The "cold" contacts were informed of the nature of the research project, its sponsorship, and its goals, given reference information for verification, and then invited to participate. The "cold" contact interviewees were also asked to make recommendations and provide contact information for others who might be interested in participating in the study.

This strategy was used in an attempt to reduce the affects of sampling bias by generating parallel social network samples. The figure below is a visual representation of a parallel social-network sampling model. The central, or first-order, node on the left is a "cold" contact or unknown individual who recommends several second-order contacts, each represented as a node within the left box. The second-order "cold" contacts then make additional recommendations for third-order contacts, and so on. The central (first-order) node on the right is a "hot" contact or a known individual who recommends several second-order contacts, each represented as a node within the right box. The second-order "hot" contacts then make recommendations for third-order contacts, and so on.

Social Network Mapping

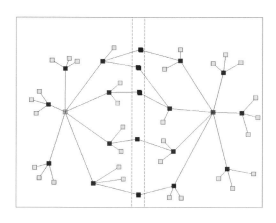

In many instances, the contacts from both social network samples overlapped or converged on specific individuals, as represented by the overlapped fourth-order nodes in the central column. There are several possible explanations for this convergence. It may indicate that there are a number of respected "thought leaders" in the Intelligence Community whom each contact believed I should interview for this project, or the convergence of nodes

---

[6] Social network sampling is also known as "snowball" sampling in sociology and psychology.

might merely serve to emphasize the small size of Intelligence Community. In any case, this approach to sampling may help to ameliorate the sampling bias inherent in qualitative research.

In addition to semi-structured interviews, both direct and participant observation data collection methods were employed. The direct observation method involved watching Intelligence Community analysts perform their tasks in both actual and training environments, recording the physical and verbal interactions they had with one another, and observing the steps used to create intelligence products. Direct observation occurred over the course of two years by observing 325 individual analysts and teams of analysts performing their specific tasks. The data collected from observing the 325 analysts were not included in the semi-structured interview data because I did not use the formal semi-structured interview process to structure those interactions. These observational data were recorded separately in field notes and used for triangulating the findings from the interviews.

The participant observation method is employed to give the researcher a "first-person" understanding of the context and nuances associated with a task and the culture in which that task occurs. Although the researcher possesses only an approximation of the knowledge and understanding of the actual practitioners of the task and their culture, this "first-person" perspective can lead the researcher to new insights and new hypotheses.

During this study, the participant observation was conducted during analytic production cycles, scenario development, and red cell exercises. This included monitoring my own analytic strategies, the analytic strategies of others as diagramed or verbalized, the physical and verbal social interactions among the participants, the environment in which the tasks occurred, and the steps used to create a final intelligence product. These data, along with notes on social dynamics, taboos, and social power, were recorded in field notes and created a separate data source for triangulation.

With modern anthropology, these data normally would be captured on film, audiotape, or in some digital format. Due to the security requirements of the Intelligence Community, however, the data were captured only in the written form of field notes. As is the case with the field notes, the identity of the interview participants will not be disclosed. This is in keeping with both the security practices of the Intelligence Community and the professional standards described in the American Anthropological Association Statement on the Confidentiality of Field Notes.[7]

The data from the interviews were analyzed using a method called interpretational analysis.[8] This approach included segmenting the interview data into

---

[7] American Anthropological Association, *Statement on the Confidentiality of Field Notes.*

analytic units (or units of meaning), developing categories, coding the analytic units into content areas, and grouping the analytic units into categories. From these categories, general trends and specific instances can be identified. As noted, the direct and participant observational data were analyzed separately in order to triangulate the findings from the interview data. The purpose of using multiple data sources for triangulation is to uncover internal inconsistencies in the data, to cross-check those inconsistencies with the available literature, and to verify the content validity for each category.

Demographics

As of this writing, 489 semi-structured interviews have been conducted with active and retired intelligence professionals, intelligence technology researchers, academics who teach the intelligence discipline or have published in it, and consumers of intelligence products.[9] Of the 489 individuals interviewed, 70-percent were newly hired, active, or retired intelligence professionals; 15-percent were academics; 11-percent were intelligence technology researchers; and the

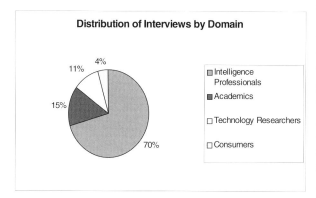

remaining four percent were policy makers or senior consumers of intelligence products. The graph here shows the distribution of interviews by percentage for each professional category.

The table below lists each professional category and the corresponding total number (N) of individuals interviewed. The intelligence professional category is further divided into three sub-groups. The "novice" sub-group includes new hires and those with less than two years of experience.[10] The "active" sub-

---

[8] Leonard Bickman and Debra Rog, *Handbook of Applied Social Research Methods;* Meredith Gall et al., *Educational Research;* Jonathan Gross, *Measuring Culture: A Paradigm for the Analysis of Social Organization;* Ernest House, *Evaluating with Validity;* Jerome Kirk and Marc Miller, *Reliability and Validity in Qualitative Research, Qualitative Research Methods, Volume 1;* Delbert Miller, *Handbook of Research Design and Social Measurement;* Michael Patton, *Qualitative Evaluation and Research Methods;* Peter Rossi and Howard Freeman, *Evaluation. A Systematic Approach.*

[9] Additional interviews are being conducted.

group includes all those currently working in the Intelligence Community with more than two years of experience. The "retired" sub-group includes those who have spent more than fifteen years in the intelligence profession and have since gone on to either full retirement or other organizations outside of the Intelligence Community.

Of the 345 intelligence professionals interviewed, 20 percent were novices, 65 percent were active, and 15 percent were retired. The active and retired sub-groups include senior managers.

Interview Categories and Numbers

Category	N
Intelligence Professionals	345
Novice	(60)
Active	(233)
Retired	(52)
Academics	73
Technology Researchers	53
Consumers	18
Total Interviewed	**489**

In order to assure anonymity for the participants, I have created broader job-related functional categories and associated the number of individuals interviewed with the broader categories rather than linking them to specific organizations within the Intelligence Community. This is in contrast to aggregating the agencies according to each agency's specific mission, process, or product. Although not an official member of the Intelligence Community, the Drug Enforcement Administration is included because of its intelligence function and resources. The table on the next page shows how I aggregated the agencies into National-Technical, Defense, and Law Enforcement-Homeland Security categories according to the professional functions of interview participants.

---

[10] The use of two years as a divide between novice and active is derived from the total amount of experience it is possible to gain in that time. See the discussion of expertise in Chapter Five.

Agency Aggregation According to Interviewee Job-type

National-Technical	Defense	Law Enforcement-Homeland Security
Central Intelligence Agency	Defense Intelligence Agency	Department of Homeland Security
National Security Agency	Army Intelligence	Federal Bureau of Investigation
National Reconnaissance Office	Air Force Intelligence	Department of Energy
National Geospatial Intelligence Agency	Navy Intelligence	Department of Treasury
Department of State (INR)	Marine Corps Intelligence	*Drug Enforcement Administration*

The figure below shows the distribution of intelligence professionals interviewed for this study according to each broader functional category. Of the 345 intelligence professionals interviewed, 214 work within the National-Technical Intelligence category, 76 in the Defense Intelligence category, and 55 in the Law Enforcement—Homeland Security category.

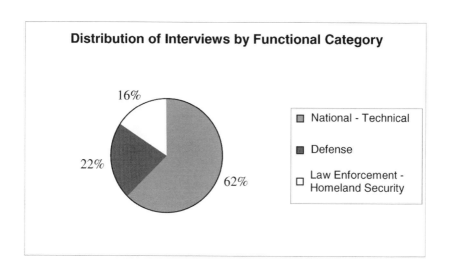

CHAPTER ELEVEN
Q-Sort Methodology

Observations always involve theory.

Edwin Hubble[1]

As described earlier, this work reflects triangulation of the data derived from the literature Q-sort, interview responses, and observations.[2] The data include 489 interviews, direct and participant observation of 325 analysts performing their jobs, participation in a variety of analytic tasks, and focus groups conducted to generate the taxonomy of variables that guided this study.

The first Q-sort of the data was aggregated according to the function of each intelligence organization, as listed in Table 1. The data were then analyzed to determine response context according to job type and to develop variable categories.

The organizational Q-sort generated the broad variable groupings used to create the second Q-sort parameters. The variable categories that emerged during the interpretive analysis of the first Q-sort of the data were compiled again, and a second Q-sort was performed based on those categories. The data was then aggregated according to categorical or variable groupings of the second Q-sort, Table 2.

The use of two separate Q-sort strategies generated the variables and then de-contextualized the data in order to find consistent trends throughout the Intelligence Community. That is, this strategy resulted in broad categories of findings that apply across many agencies. In those cases where interview and

---

[1] Edwin Hubble discovered the first evidence to support the Big Bang theory that the universe is expanding and that the Milky Way is not the only galaxy in the universe. He also developed the Hubble Galaxy Classification System and Hubble's Law (the farther away a galaxy is from Earth, the faster its motion away from Earth). Edwin Hubble, *The Realm of the Nebulae*.

[2] William Stephenson, *The Study of Behavior: Q-Technique and its Methodology*.

observational data could have been sorted into several categories, I based the placement of the data on the question that generated the interview response.

Table 1. Q-Sort 1. Data Grouping According to Organizational Function.

National – Technical	Defense	Law Enforcement – Homeland Security
Central Intelligence Agency	Defense Intelligence Agency	Department of Homeland Security
National Security Agency	Army Intelligence	Federal Bureau of Investigation
National Reconnaissance Office	Air Force Intelligence	Department of Energy
National Geospatial Intelligence Agency	Navy Intelligence	Department of the Treasury
Department of State (INR)	Marine Corps Intelligence	*Drug Enforcement Administration*

In several instances throughout the text, the quotes that were used may well fit in a number of other categories. Once the data were sorted by variable, the coding and context identifier notes were removed from all data in order to assure participant anonymity, in keeping with the American Anthropological Association *Code of Ethics*, section III, A.[3]

Table 2. Q-Sort 2. Data Grouping According to Variable Categories.

Time Constraints	Analytic Methods	Organizational Norms	Analytic Identity	Analytic Training
Products	Tradecraft	Taboos	Reportorial	Formal
Interactions	Science	Biases	Academic	Informal

The quotes that appear throughout the text are exemplars from each variable category and indicate trends found in the data-set. Although the exemplar quotes are not universal, nor are they necessarily subject to generalization, they do represent consistent findings from the interview and observation data. Utilizing this approach to develop theory is similar to the method in which grounded theory is employed in sociology, specifically, using grounded data to generate theory rather than using some a priori technique. The significant advantage to this approach is that the theory is directly tied to data, providing it additional validity. Another advantage is that the individuals who allowed me to interview and observe them are given some voice in the final product by way of direct quotes, which also provides some qualitative context.

---

[3] American Anthropological Association, *Code of Ethics of the American Anthropological Association.*

CHAPTER TWELVE

The "File-Drawer" Problem and Calculation of Effect Size

The file-drawer problem appears to have two causes: the reluctance of researchers to report their null results and the reluctance of professional journal editors to include studies whose results fail to reach statistical significance. Such studies remain in the "file-drawers" of the researchers. How much would these inaccessible studies affect the results of our meta-analysis? The answer seems to be not much.[1]

Effect Size - Difference Between Two Means

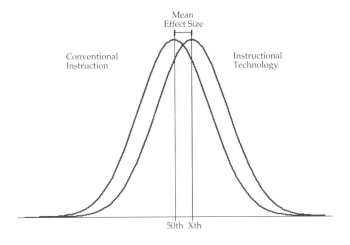

[1] Gene Glass, and Barry McGaw, "Choice of the Metric for Effect Size in Meta-Analysis"; Larry Hedges, "Estimation of Effect Size from a Series of Independent Experiments"; Larry Hedges and Ingram Olkin, "Vote-Counting Methods in Research Synthesis."

Effect size is usually defined as the difference between the means of two groups divided by the standard deviation of the control group $\left(\Delta = \dfrac{\overline{X}_e - \overline{X}_c}{\sigma_c} \right)$.[2]

Effect sizes calculated in this way estimate the difference between two group means measured in control group standard deviations as seen in the figure above. Glass et al. suggest that the choice of the denominator is critical and that choices other than the control group standard deviation are defensible.[3] However, they endorse the standard choice of using the control group standard deviation.

Alternatively, Hedges and Olkin show that, for every effect size, both the bias and variance of its estimate are smaller when standard deviation is obtained by pooling the sample variance of two groups instead of using the control group standard deviation by itself.[4] An effect size based on a pooled standard deviation estimates the difference between two group means measured in standard deviations estimated for the full population from which both experimental and control groups are drawn: $\left(g = \dfrac{\overline{X}_e - \overline{X}_c}{S} \right)$,[5] where

S is the pooled standard deviation: $S = \sqrt{\dfrac{(N_e - 1)(S_e)^2 + (N_c - 1)(S_c)^2}{N_e + N_c - 2}}$.[6]

Most commentators suggest that effect sizes can be treated as descriptive statistics and entered into standard tests for statistical significance. Hedges and Olkin have shown that the error variance around estimates of effect size is inversely proportional to the sample size of the studies from which the effect sizes are drawn. If the effect size in any review is drawn from studies employing widely different sample sizes, then the heterogeneity of variance among effect sizes prohibits their use in conventional t-tests, analyses of variance, and other inferential tests. This is the case in most of these reviews; therefore, effect sizes reported in this study are treated only with descriptive statistics.

The effect sizes for computer-based training range from 0.20 to 0.46 depending on the population.[7] The effect size for distance instruction (television) is

---

[2] Δ = Glass's Effect Size, $\overline{X}_e$ = Experimental Mean, $\overline{X}_c$ = Control Mean, σ_c = Control Standard Deviation

[3] Gene Glass, Barry McGaw and Mary Lee Smith, *Meta-Analysis in Social Research.*

[4] Larry Hedges and Ingram Olkin, *Statistical Methods for Meta-Analysis.*

[5] g=Hedge's Effect Size, S=Hedge's Pooled Standard Deviation

[6] Ne=Number of experimental subjects, Nc=Number of control subjects, Se=Standard deviation of experimental group, Sc=Standard deviation of control group

0.15 and for interactive videodiscs, the effect sizes range from 0.17 to 0.66 depending on the population.[8] The effect size for flight simulation is 0.54 and the effect size for tutorials range from 0.25 to 0.41 depending on the presentation of the tutorial material.[9]

Although the effect sizes for instructional technology range from 0.15 to 0.66 standard deviations, they all report favorable findings when compared to conventional instruction. There are many possible explanations for the differences in instructional technology effectiveness; it might be the result of population differences, system differences, interactivity or individualization. From a purely utilitarian point of view, the reason may not be all that important. If, at the very least, using instructional technology forces the producer to rethink the content of the course to match the delivery system, then

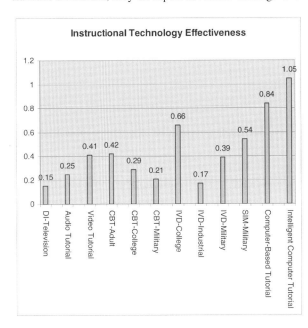

revisiting the pedagogy may be enough to produce the positive effect sizes. Whatever reason for the changes in effectiveness, the use of instructional technology saves instructional time, overhead costs, and results in a higher level of achievement for the students in a variety of domains.

---

[7] The abbreviations in figure one: CBT=Computer Based Training, DI=Distance Instruction, IVD=Interactive Video Disc, SIM=Simulation. More than 300 research studies were used to develop these effect sizes, see Chen-Lin Kulik., James Kulik and Barbara Shwalb, "Effectiveness of Computer-Based Adult Education: A Meta-Analysis"; Chen-Lin Kulik and James Kulik, "Effectiveness of Computer-Based Education in Colleges"; Rob Johnston and J. Dexter Fletcher, *A Meta-Analysis of the Effectiveness of Computer-Based Training for Military Instruction*.

[8] Godwin Chu and Wilbur Schramm, *Learning from Television*; J. Dexter Fletcher *Effectiveness and Cost of Interactive Videodisc Instruction in Defense Training and Education*; J. Dexter Fletcher, "Computer-Based Instruction: Costs and Effectiveness."

[9] R. T. Hays, J. W. Jacobs, C. Prince and E. Salas, "Flight Simulator Training Effectiveness: A Meta-Analysis"; Peter Cohen, James Kulik and Chen-Lin Kulik, "Educational Outcomes of Tutoring."

APPENDIX

Selected Literature

Intelligence Tools and Techniques

Jerome K. Clauser and Sandra M. Weir, *Intelligence Research Methodology: An Introduction to Techniques and Procedures for Conducting Research in Defense Intelligence* (Washington, DC: US Defense Intelligence School, 1976).

Stanley Feder, "FACTIONS and Policon: New Ways to Analyze Politics," (1987) in H. Bradford Westerfield, ed., *Inside CIA's Private World: Declassified Articles from the Agency's Internal Journal* (New Haven: Yale University Press, 1995).

Craig Fleisher and Babette Bensoussan, *Strategic and Competitive Analysis. Methods and Techniques for Analyzing Business Competition* (Upper Saddle River, NJ: Pearson Education, 2003).

Leonard Fuld, *The New Competitor Intelligence. The Complete Resource for Finding, Analyzing, and Using Information About Your Competitors* (New York: John Wiley & Sons, 1995).

Ronald Garst, ed., *A Handbook of Intelligence Analysis*, 2nd ed (Washington, DC: Defense Intelligence College, 1989).

R. Hopkins, *Warnings of Revolution: A Case Study of El Salvador* (Washington, DC: Center for the Study of Intelligence, 1980) TR 80-100012.

Morgan Jones, *The Thinker's Toolkit: 14 Powerful Techniques for Problem Solving* (New York, NY: Times Business, 1998).

Larry Kahaner, *Competitive Intelligence. How to Gather, Analyze, and Use Information to Move Your Business to the Top* (New York: Touchstone, Simon and Schuster, 1996).

Jonathan Lockwood and K. Lockwood, "The Lockwood Analytical Method for Prediction (LAMP)," *Defense Intelligence Journal* 3, no. 2 (1994): 47–74.

Douglas J. MacEachin, et al., *The Tradecraft of Analysis: Challenge and Change in the CIA* (Washington, DC: Consortium for the Study of Intelligence, 1994).

Don McDowell, *Strategic Intelligence: A Handbook for Practitioners, Managers and Users* (Canberra, Australia: Istana Enterprises, 1998).

Marilyn Peterson, *Applications in Criminal Analysis* (Westport, CT: Greenwood Press, 1995).

———, Bob Morehouse, and Richard Wright, eds. *Intelligence 2000: Revising the Basic Elements* (Sacramento CA: LEIU and IALEIA, 2000).

John Pierce, "Some Mathematical Methods for Intelligence Analysis," *Studies in Intelligence* 21 (Summer 1977, declassified): 1–19.

John Prescott and Stephen Miller, eds. *Proven Strategies in Competitive Intelligence* (New York: John Wiley & Sons, 2001).

Edwin Sapp, "Decision Trees," *Studies in Intelligence* 18 (Winter 1974, declassified): 45–57.

David Schum, *The Evidential Foundations of Probabilistic Reasoning* (Evanston, IL: Northwestern University Press, 1994).

Jack Zlotnick, "Bayes' Theorem for Intelligence Analysis," (1972), in H. Bradford Westerfield, ed. *Inside CIA's Private World: Declassified Articles from the Agency's Internal Journal* (New Haven: Yale University Press, 1995).

Cognitive Processes and Intelligence

Edgar Johnson, *Effects of Data Source Reliability on Inference* (Alexandria, VA: Army Research Institute for the Behavioral and Social Sciences, Technical Paper #251, 1974).

Robert Mathams, "The Intelligence Analyst's Notebook," in Douglas Dearth and R. Thomas Goodden, eds., *Strategic Intelligence: Theory and Application*, 2nd ed. (Washington, DC: Joint Military Intelligence College, 1995).

Avi Shlaim, "Failures in National Intelligence Estimates: The Case of the Yom Kippur War," *World Politics* 28, no. 3 (1976): 348–80.

Tools and Techniques as Cognitive Processes

Bruce D. Berkowitz and Allan E. Goodman, *Best Truth: Intelligence in the Information Age* (New Haven: Yale University Press, 2000).

———, and Allan E. Goodman, *Strategic Intelligence for American National Security* (Princeton: Princeton University Press, 1989).

Sherman Kent, "Words of Estimative Probability," *Sherman Kent and the Board of National Estimates: Collected Essays* (Washington, DC: Center for the Study of Intelligence, 1994).

Lisa Krizan, *Intelligence Essentials for Everyone* (Washington, DC: Joint Military Intelligence College, 1999).

Intelligence Analysis as Individual Cognitive Process

Alexander Butterfield, *The Accuracy of Intelligence Assessment: Bias, Perception, and Judgment in Analysis and Decision* (Newport, RI: Naval War College, 1993).

Richards J. Heuer, Jr., *Psychology of Intelligence Analysis* (Washington, DC: Center for the Study of Intelligence, 1999).

Robert Jervis, *Perception and Misperception in International Politics* (Princeton: Princeton University Press, 1977).

Ephraim Kam, *Surprise Attack: The Victim's Perspective* (Cambridge, MA: Harvard University Press, 1988).

Geraldine Krotow, *The Impact of Cognitive Feedback on the Performance of Intelligence Analysts* (Monterey, CA: Naval Postgraduate School, 1992).

Mark Lowenthal, *Intelligence: From Secrets to Policy* (Washington, DC: CQ, 2000).

David Moore, Creating Intelligence: Evidence and Inference in the Analysis Process. Unpublished Masters Thesis (Washington DC: Joint Military Intelligence College, 2002).

J. R. Thompson, R. Hopf-Weichel, and R. Geiselman, *The Cognitive Bases of Intelligence Analysis* (Alexandria, VA: Army Research Institute, Research Report 1362, 1984).

Error

Daniela Busse and Chris Johnson "Using a Cognitive Theoretical Framework to Support Accident Analysis," in *Proceedings of the Working Group on Human Error, Safety, and System Development* (Seattle, WA: International Federation for Information Processing, 1998, 36–43).

Peter Fishburn, *Utility Theory for Decision Making* (New York: John Wiley, 1970).

Paul Fitts and Michael Posner, *Human Performance* (Belmont, CA: Brooks Cole, 1967).

John Hammond, Ralph Keeney, and Howard Raiffa, "The Hidden Traps in Decision Making," *Harvard Business Review*, Sept.– Oct. 1998: 47–58.

Hede Helfrich, "Human Reliability from a Social-Psychological Perspective," *International Journal Human-Computer Studies* 50 (1999): 193–212.

Erik Hollnagel, "The Phenotype of Erroneous Actions," *International Journal of Man-Machine Studies* 39 (1993): 1–32.

Daniel Kahneman and Amos Tversky, "Prospect Theory: An Analysis of Decision Under Risk," *Econometrica* 47, no. 2 (1979): 263–91.

Duncan Luce and Howard Raiffa, "Utility Theory" in Paul Moser, ed. *Rationality in Action: Contemporary Approaches* (New York: Cambridge University Press, 1990).

Judith Orasanu and Lynne Martin, "Errors in Aviation Decision Making: A Factor in Accidents and Incidents" in *Proceedings of the Working Group on Human Error, Safety, and System Development* (Seattle, WA: International Federation for Information Processing, 1998, 100–107).

James Reason, *Human Error* (New York: Cambridge University Press, 1990).

John Senders and Neville Moray, *Human Error: Cause, Prediction and Reduction* (Hillsdale, NJ: Earlbaum, 1991).

Neville Stanton and Sarah Stevenage, "Learning to Predict Human Error: Issues of Acceptability, Reliability and Validity," *Ergonomics* 41, no. 11 (1998): 1737–56.

Language and Cognition

Terry K. Au, "Chinese and English Counterfactuals: The Sapir-Whorf Hypothesis Revisited," *Cognition* 15 (1983): 155-187.

Alfred Bloom, *The Linguistic Shaping of Thought: A Study in the Impact of Language on Thinking in China and the West* (Hillsdale, NJ: Lawrence Erlbaum Associates, 1981).

Lera Boroditsky, "Does Language Shape Thought? Mandarin and English Speakers' Conceptions of Time," *Cognitive Psychology* 43 (2001):1–22.

Ernest Cassirer, "Le Langage et le Monde des Objets," *Journal de Psychologie Nomale et Pathologique* 30, 1(4) (1933): 18–44.

John Gumperz and Dell Hymes, *Directions in Sociolinguistics: The Ethnography of Communication* (Oxford: B. Blackwell, 1986).

———, and Stephen Levinson, *Rethinking Linguistic Relativity* (Cambridge: Cambridge University Press, 1996).

Harry Hoijer, "The Relation of Language to Culture" in Alfred Kroeber, ed. *Anthropology Today* (Chicago: University of Chicago Press, 1953).

Wilhelm von Humboldt *"Uber die Verschiedenheit des Menschlichen Sprachbaues"* in B. Bohr, ed. *Gesammelte Schriften* (Berlin: Verlag, 1907).

Earl Hunt and Franca Agnoli, "The Whorfian Hypothesis. A Cognitive Psychology Perspective," *Psychological Review* 98, no. 3 (1991): 377–89.

Dell Hymes, ed. *Language in Culture and Society: A Reader in Linguistics and Anthropology* (New York: Harper and Row, 1977).

Penny Lee, *The Whorf Theory Complex: A Critical Reconstruction* (Amsterdam: Benjamins, 1996).

Lisa Liu, "Reasoning Counterfactually in Chinese: Are There any Obstacles?" *Cognition* 21 (1985): 239–70.

John Lucy, *Grammatical Categories and Cognition* (Cambridge: Cambridge University Press, 1992) and *Language Diversity and Thought* (Cambridge: Cambridge University Press, 1992).

George Miller and Philip Johnson-Laird, *Language and Perception* (Cambridge, MA: Harvard University Press, 1976).

Richard Nisbett and Ara Norenzayan, "Culture and Cognition" in Douglas Medin and Hal Pashler, eds. *Stevens' Handbook of Experimental Psychology*, 3rd ed. (New York: John Wiley & Sons, 2002).

Edward Sapir, *Language* (New York: Harcourt Brace, 1949).

Jost Trier, *Der deutsche Wortschatz im Sinnbezirk des Verstandes* (Heidelberg: Carl Winter, 1931).

Leo Weisgerber, *Vom Weltbild der Deutschen Sprache* (Dusseldorf: Padagogischer Verlag Schwann, 1953).

Benjamin Whorf, *Language, Thought, and Reality* (New York: John Wiley, 1956).

BIBLIOGRAPHY

Published Sources

Akin, Omer. *Models of Architectural Knowledge.* London: Pion, 1980.

Allen, Charles, *Comments of the Associate Director of Central Intelligence for Collection at a Public Seminar on Intelligence at Harvard University,* spring 2000. (<http://pirp.harvard.edu/pdf-blurb.asp? id+518>.)

Allison, Graham T. *Essence of Decision: Explaining the Cuban Missile Crisis.* Boston: Little, Brown and Company, 1971.

American Anthropological Association. *Code of Ethics of the American Anthropological Association.* Arlington, VA, 1998. (http://www.aaanet.org/committees/ethics/ethcode.htm.)

————. *Statement on the Confidentiality of Field Notes.* Arlington, VA, 2003. (http://www.aaanet.org/stmts/fieldnotes.htm.)

American College of Radiology. Written communications between staff and Johnston, 2002.

Arvey, Richard D., and James E. Campion. "The Employment Interview: A Summary of Recent Research," *Personnel Psychology* 35 (1982): 281–322.

Ashcraft, M.H. *Fundamentals of Cognition.* New York: Addison Wesley Longman, 1998.

Atkinson, R. C., and H. A. Wilson. *Computer-Assisted Instruction: A Book of Readings,* New York: Academic Press, 1969.

Au, Terry K. "Chinese and English Counterfactuals: The Sapir-Whorf Hypothesis Revisited," *Cognition* 15 (1983): 155–87.

Barr, A., M. Beard, and R. C. Atkinson. "A Rationale and Description of a CAI Program to Teach the BASIC Programming Language." *Instructional Science* 4 (1975): 1–31.

Bayes, Thomas. "An Essay Toward Solving a Problem in the Doctrine of Chances," *Philosophical Transactions of the Royal Society of London* 53: 370–418. (http://plato.stanford.edu/entries/bayes-theorum/#Bib.)

Ben-Israel, Isaac. "Philosophy and Methodology of Intelligence: The Logic of Estimate Process," *Intelligence and National Security* 4, no. 4 (1989): 660–718.

Ben-Zvi, Abraham. "The Study of Surprise Attacks," *British Journal of International Studies* 5 (1979).

Berkowitz, Bruce D., and Allan E. Goodman. *Best Truth: Intelligence in the Information Age*. New Haven, CT: Yale University Press, 2000.

———. *Strategic Intelligence for American National Security*. Princeton, NJ: Princeton University Press, 1989.

Bernard, Russell. *Research Methods in Anthropology: Qualitative and Quantitative Approaches*. Thousand Oaks, CA: Sage, 1994.

Betts, Richard K. "Policy-Makers and Intelligence Analysts: Love, Hate or Indifference," *Intelligence and National Security* 3, no. 1 (January 1988): 184–89.

———. *Surprise Attack*. Washington, DC: The Brookings Institution, 1982.

Bickman, Leonard, and Debra Rog. *Handbook of Applied Social Research Methods*. Thousand Oaks, CA: Sage, 1997.

Bloom, Alfred. *The Linguistic Shaping of Thought: A Study in the Impact of Language on Thinking in China and the West*. Hillsdale, NJ: Lawrence Erlbaum Associates, 1981.

Bloom, Benjamin S., ed. *Taxonomy of Educational Objectives: The Classification of Educational Goals: Handbook I, Cognitive Domain*. New York: Longmans, Green, 1956.

———. "The 2 Sigma Problem: The Search for Methods of Group Instruction as Effective as One-to-One Tutoring," *Educational Researcher*, 13 (1984): 4–16.

Boas, Franz. "An Anthropologist's Credo," *The Nation* 147 (1938): 201–4.

Bogdan, Robert. *Participant Observation in Organizational Settings*. Syracuse, NY: Syracuse University Press, 1972.

Boroditsky, Lera. "Does Language Shape Thought? Mandarin and English Speakers' Conceptions of Time," *Cognitive Psychology* 43 (2001): 1–22.

Bourdieu, Pierre. "The Forms of Capital" in John Richardson, ed. *Handbook of Theory and Research for the Sociology of Education*. New York: Greenwood Press, 1986.

Brei, William. *Getting Intelligence Right: The Power of Logical Procedure*. Washington, DC: Joint Military Intelligence College, 1996.

Brinberg, David, and Joseph McGrath. *Validity and the Research Process*. Beverly Hills, CA: Sage, 1985.

Brown, J.S., R.R. Burton, and J. DeKleer. "Pedagogical, Natural Language, and Knowledge Engineering in SOPHIE I, II, and III" in D. Sleeman and J.S. Brown, eds. *Intelligent Tutoring Systems*, New York: Academic Press, 1982.

Busse, Daniela, and Chris Johnson. "Using a Cognitive Theoretical Framework to Support Accident Analysis," *Proceedings of the Working Group on Human Error, Safety, and System Development*. Seattle, WA: International Federation for Information Processing, 1998, 36–43.

Butterfield, Alexander. *The Accuracy of Intelligence Assessment: Bias, Perception, and Judgment in Analysis and Decision*. Newport, RI: Naval War College, 1993, AD-A266.

Camerer, Colin, and Eric Johnson. "The Process-Performance Paradox in Expert Judgment: How Can Experts Know so Much and Predict so Badly?" in K. Anders Ericsson and Jacqui Smith, eds. *Toward a General Theory of Expertise: Prospects and Limit.* Cambridge: Cambridge University Press, 1991.

Cannon-Bowers, Janis, Eduardo Salas, and S. Converse. "Shared Mental Models in Expert Team Decision Making" in J. N. John Castellan, ed. *Current Issues in Individual and Group Decision Making.* Hillsdale, NY: Lawrence Erlbaum Associates, 1983.

Capra, Fritjof. "Criteria of Systems Thinking," *Futures,* October 1985: 475–78.

Carbonell, J. R. "AI in CAI: An Artificial Intelligence Approach to Computer-Assisted Instruction" in *IEEE Transactions on Man-Machine Systems,* 11 (1970): 190–202; J. D. Fletcher and M. R. Rockway loc. cit.

Carmines, Edward, and Richard Zeller. *Reliability and Validity Assessment.* Newbury Park, CA: Sage, 1991.

Cartwright, Dorwin, and Alvin Zander. *Group Dynamics: Research and Theory.* New York: Harper & Row, 1960.

Cascio, Wayne F. *Applied Psychology in Human Resource Management.* 5th ed. Englewood Cliffs, NJ: Prentice Hall, 1998.

Cassirer, Ernest. "Le Langage et le Monde des Objets," *Journal de Psychologie Nomale et Pathologique* 30, 1(4) (1933): 18–44.

Central Intelligence Agency. *A Consumer's Guide to Intelligence.* Washington, DC: Central Intelligence Agency, 1993.

———. *Factbook on Intelligence* (http://www.cia.gov/cia/publications/fact-tell/index.html.)

Chambers, Erve. *Applied Anthropology: A Practical Guide.* Prospect Heights, IL: Waveland Press, 1989.

Chase, William G. "Spatial Representations of Taxi Drivers" in Don Rogers and John Slobada, eds. *Acquisition of Symbolic Skills.* New York: Plenum, 1983.

———, and Herbert Simon. "Perception in Chess," *Cognitive Psychology* 4 (1973): 55–81.

———, and K. Anders Ericsson. "Skill and Working Memory" in Gordon Bower, ed. *The Psychology of Learning and Motivation.* New York: Academic Press, 1982.

Chi, Michelene, Robert Glaser, and Ernest Rees. "Expertise in Problem Solving" in Robert Sternberg, ed. *Advances in the Psychology of Human Intelligence.* Hillsdale, NJ: Lawrence Erlbaum Associates, 1982.

———, Paul Feltovich, and Robert Glaser. "Categorization and Representation of Physics Problems by Experts and Novices," *Cognitive Science* 5 (1981): 121–25.

Chu, Godwin, and Wilbur Schramm. *Learning from Television: What the Research Says.* Stanford, CA: Stanford University, Institute for Communication Research, 1968.

Clauser, Jerome K., and Sandra M. Weir. *Intelligence Research Methodology: An Introduction to Techniques and Procedures for Conducting Research in Defense Intelligence.* Washington, DC: US Defense Intelligence School, 1976.

Cline, Marjorie, Carla Christiansen, and Judith Fontaine. *Scholar's Guide to Intelligence Literature: Bibliography of the Russell J. Bowen Collection.* Frederick, MD: University Publications of America, 1983.

Coch, Lester, and John French. "Overcoming Resistance to Change," Dorwin Cartwright and Alvin Zander, eds. *Group Dynamics: Research and Theory.* New York: Harper & Row, 1960.

Cohen, Peter, James Kulik, and Chen-Lin Kulik. "Educational Outcomes of Tutoring: A Meta-Analysis of Findings," *American Educational Research Journal* 19 (1982): 237–48.

Cushman, Philip. *Constructing the Self, Constructing America.* Reading, MA: Addison-Wesley, 1995.

Davis, Jack. "Combating Mindset," *Studies in Intelligence* 35 (Winter 1991): 13–18.

Dawes, Robyn. Written communications between Dawes and Johnston, 2002.
———. "A Case Study of Graduate Admissions: Application of Three Principles of Human Decision Making," *American Psychologist* 26 (1971): 180–88.
———, David Faust, and Paul Meehl. "Clinical Versus Actuarial Judgment," *Science* 243 (1989): 1668–74.

Dearth, Douglas, and R. Thomas Goodden, eds. *Strategic Intelligence: Theory and Application*, 2nd ed. Washington, DC: Joint Military Intelligence College, 1995.

Denzin, Norman, and Yvonna Lincoln, eds. *Handbook of Qualitative Research.* Thousand Oaks, CA: Sage, 1994.

Deutsch, Morton. "The Effects of Cooperation and Competition Upon Group Process" in Dorwin Cartwright and Alvin Zander, eds. *Group Dynamics: Research and Theory.* New York: Harper & Row, 1960.

Duffy, T. M., and D. H. Jonassen, eds. *Constructivism and the Technology of Instruction: A Conversation.* Hillsdale, NJ: Erlbaum, 1992.

Eco, Umberto. *A Theory of Semiotics.* Bloomington, IN: Indiana University Press, 1979.

Egan, D., and B. Schwartz. "Chunking in Recall of Symbolic Drawings," *Memory and Cognition* 7 (1979): 149–58.

Elkins, Dan. *An Intelligence Resource Manager's Guide.* Washington, DC: Joint Military Intelligence College, 1997.

Endsley, M.R. "Design and Evaluation for Situation Awareness Enhancement," *Proceedings of Human Factors Society 32nd Annual Meeting*, Santa Monica, CA: Human Factors Society, 1988.

Ervin, Alexander. *Applied Anthropology. Tools and Perspectives for Contemporary Practice*. Boston: Allyn and Bacon, 2000.

Evans, Jonathan St. B. T. *Bias in Human Reasoning: Causes and Consequences*. Hove, UK: Lawrence Erlbaum Associates, 1989.

Fandt, Patricia, W. Richardson, and H. Conner. "The Impact of Goal Setting on Team Simulation Experience," *Simulation and Gaming* 21, no. 4 (1990): 411–22.

Feder, Stanley. "FACTIONS and Policon: New Ways to Analyze Politics," (1987), in H. Bradford Westerfield, ed. *Inside CIA's Private World: Declassified Articles from the Agency's Internal Journal*. New Haven, CT: Yale University Press, 1995.

Feldman, Daniel C. "The Multiple Socialization of Organization Members." *Academy of Management Review* 6, no. 2 (1981): 309–18.

Feldman, Tine, and Susan Assaf. *Social Capital: Conceptual Frameworks and Empirical Evidence. An Annotated Bibliography*. Social Capital Initiative Working Paper No. 5. Washington, DC: The World Bank, 1999.

Festinger, Leon. "Informal Social Communication" in Dorwin Cartwright and Alvin Zander, eds. *Group Dynamics: Research and Theory*. New York: Harper & Row, 1960.

Fishburn, Peter. *Utility Theory for Decision Making*. New York. John Wiley, 1970.

Fitts, Paul, and Michael Posner. *Human Performance*. Belmont, CA: Brooks Cole, 1967.

Flavell, J.H. "Metacognitive Aspects of Problem Solving" in L. Resnick, ed. *The Nature of Intelligence*. Hillsdale, NJ: Lawrence Erlbaum Associates, 1976.

Fleisher, Craig, and Babette Bensoussan. *Strategic and Competitive Analysis. Methods and Techniques for Analyzing Business Competition*. Upper Saddle River, NJ: Pearson Education, 2003.

Fleishman, Edwin, and Marilyn Quaintance. *Taxonomies of Human Performance*. New York: Academic Press, 1984.

Fletcher, J. Dexter. "Computer-Based Instruction: Costs and Effectiveness" in Andrew Sage, ed. *Concise Encyclopedia of Information Processing in Systems and Organizations*. Elmsford, NY: Pergamon Press, 1990.

———. *Effectiveness and Cost of Interactive Videodisc Instruction in Defense Training and Education*. Alexandria, VA: Institute for Defense Analyses, 1990, IDA P-2372.

———. "Evidence for Learning From Technology-Assisted Instruction" in Harold F. O'Neil, Jr. and Ray Perez, eds. *Technology Applications in Education: A Learning View*. Hillsdale, NJ: Lawrence Erlbaum Associates, 2003.

————. *Technology, the Columbus Effect, and the Third Revolution in Learning*. Alexandria, VA: Institute for Defense Analyses, 2001, D-2562.

————, and Rob Johnston. "Effectiveness and Cost Benefits of Computer-Based Decision Aids for Equipment Maintenance," *Computers in Human Behavior* 18 (2002): 717–28.

————, and M. R. Rockway. "Computer-based Training in the Military" in J. A. Ellis, ed. *Military Contributions to Instructional Technology*. New York: Praeger Publishers, 1986.

Folker, Robert D. *Intelligence Analysis in Theater Joint Intelligence Centers: An Experiment in Applying Structured Methods*. Washington, DC: Joint Military Intelligence College, Occasional Paper #7, 2000.

Ford, Harold. *Estimative Intelligence: The Purposes and Problems of National Intelligence Estimating*. Lanham, MD: University Press of America, 1993.

Freud, Sigmund. "A Philosophy of Life: Lecture 35," *New Introductory Lectures on Psycho-Analysis*. London: Hogarth Press, 1933.

Fries, J., et al. "Assessment of Radiologic Progression in Rheumatoid Arthritis: A Randomized, Controlled Trial," *Arthritis Rheum* 29, no. 1 (1986): 1–9.

Fuld, Leonard. *The New Competitor Intelligence: The Complete Resource for Finding, Analyzing, and Using Information About Your Competitors*. New York: John Wiley & Sons, 1995.

Galanter, E., ed. *Automatic Teaching: The State of the Art*. New York: John Wiley & Sons, 1959.

Gall, Meredith, Walter Borg, and Joyce Gall. *Educational Research*, Sixth Edition. White Plains, NY: Longman, 1996.

Garst, Ronald, ed. *A Handbook of Intelligence Analysis*, 2nd ed. Washington, DC: Defense Intelligence College, 1989.

Geertz, Clifford. *The Interpretation of Cultures*. New York: Basic Books, 1973.

Giddens, Anthony. *Modernity and Self-Identity*. Stanford, CA: Stanford University Press, 1991.

Glaser, Barney, and Anselm Strauss. *Discovery of Grounded Theory: Strategies for Qualitative Research*. Hawthorne, NY: Aldine de Gruyter, 1967.

————. *Theoretical Sensitivity: Advances in the Methodology of Grounded Theory*. Mill Valley, CA: Sociology Press, 1978.

————. *Basics of Grounded Theory Analysis: Emergence vs. Forcing*. Mill Valley, CA: Sociology Press, 1992.

Glass, Gene. "Primary, Secondary, and Meta-Analysis of Research." *Educational Researcher* 5 (1976): 3–8.

————, and Barry McGaw. "Choice of the Metric for Effect Size in Meta-Analysis." *American Educational Research Journal* 17 (1980): 325–7.

————, Barry McGaw, and Mary Lee Smith. *Meta-Analysis in Social Research*. New York: Sage, 1981.

Godson, Roy, ed. *Comparing Foreign Intelligence: The U.S., the USSR, the U.K. and the Third World.* Washington, DC: Pergamon-Brassey, 1988.

Goldberg, Lewis. "Simple Models or Simple Processes? Some Research on Clinical Judgments," *American Psychologist* 23 (1968): 483–96.

———. "Man versus Model of Man: A Rationale, Plus Some Evidence, for a Method of Improving on Clinical Inferences," *Psychological Bulletin* 73 (1970): 422–32.

Goldgeier, James M. "Psychology and Security," *Security Studies* 6, no. 4 (1997): 137–66.

Gott, Sherrie, P.R.S. Kane, and Alan Lesgold. *Tutoring for Transfer of Technical Competence.* Brooks AFB, TX: Armstrong Laboratory, Human Resources Directorate, 1995, AL/HR-TP-1995-0002.

Graesser, A.C., M.A. Gernsbacher, and S. Goldman, eds. *Handbook of Discourse Processes,* Mahwah, NJ: Lawrence Erlbaum Associates, 2003.

———, and Natalie Person. "Question-Asking During Tutoring." *American Educational Research Journal* 31 (1994): 104–37.

Greenberg, Jerald, and Robert A. Baron. *Behavior in Organizations: The Human Side of Work.* Upper Saddle River, NJ: Prentice-Hall, 2002.

Grimes, Barbara, ed. *Ethnologue,* 14th ed. Dallas, TX: Summer Institute of Linguistics, 2000.

Gross, Jonathan. *Measuring Culture: A Paradigm for the Analysis of Social Organization.* New York: Columbia University Press, 1985.

Grove, William, and Paul Meehl. "Comparative Efficiency of Informal (Subjective, Impressionistic) and Formal (Mechanical, Algorithmic) Prediction Procedures: The Clinical-Statistical Controversy," *Psychology, Public Policy, and Law* 2, no. 2 (1996): 293–323.

Gumperz, John, and Dell Hymes. *Directions in Sociolinguistics: The Ethnography of Communication.* Oxford: B. Blackwell, 1986.

———, and Stephen Levinson. *Rethinking Linguistic Relativity.* Cambridge: Cambridge University Press, 1996.

Hacker, D.J. *Metacognition: Definitions and Empirical Foundations* [On-line report]. Memphis, TN: The University of Memphis, 2001. Retrieved 30 May 2001 from the World Wide Web. (http://www.psyc.memphis.edu/trg/meta.htm.)

Hammond, John, Ralph Keeney, and Howard Raiffa. "The Hidden Traps in Decision Making." *Harvard Business Review,* September–October 1998, 47–58.

Harvey, J., and C. Boettger. "Improving Communication Within a Managerial Workgroup," *Journal of Applied Behavioral Science* 7 (1971): 164–74.

Hayes, J.R. *The Complete Problem Solver,* Philadelphia: The Franklin Institute, 1981.

Hays, R. T., et al. "Flight Simulator Training Effectiveness: A Meta-Analysis." *Military Psychology* 4, no. 2 (1992): 63–74.

Hedges, Larry. "Estimation of Effect Size From a Series of Independent Experiments," *Psychological Bulletin*, 7 (1982): 119–37.

———, and Ingram Olkin. "Vote-Counting Methods in Research Synthesis," *Psychological Bulletin* 88 (1980): 359–69.

———, and Ingram Olkin. *Statistical Methods for Meta-Analysis*. New York: Academic Press, 1985.

Helfrich, Hede. "Human Reliability From a Social-Psychological Perspective," *International Journal Human-Computer Studies* 50 (1999): 193–212.

Hesketh, Beryl, and Stephen Bochner. "Technological Change in a Multicultural Context: Implications for Training and Career Planning" in Marvin Dunnette and Leaetta Hough, eds. *Handbook of Industrial and Organizational Psychology*. Palo Alto, CA: Consulting Psychologists Press, 1994.

Heuer, Richards J., Jr. *Psychology of Intelligence Analysis*. Washington, DC: Center for the Study of Intelligence, 1999.

Hewitt, John P. *Self and Society,* 7th ed. Boston: Allyn and Bacon, 1997.

Hinchman, Lewis P., and Sandra K. Hinchman, eds. *Memory, Identity, Community*. Albany, NY: State University of New York Press, 1997.

Hoijer, Harry. "The Relation of Language to Culture" in Alfred Kroeber, ed. *Anthropology Today*. Chicago: University of Chicago Press, 1953.

Hollnagel, Erik. "The Phenotype of Erroneous Actions." *International Journal of Man-Machine Studies* 39 (1993): 1–32.

Hopkins, R. *Warnings of Revolution: A Case Study of El Salvador*. Washington, DC: Center for the Study of Intelligence, 1980, TR 80-100012.

House, Ernest. *Evaluating with Validity*. Beverly Hills, CA: Sage, 1980.

Hubble, Edwin. *The Realm of the Nebulae*. New Haven, CT: Yale University Press, 1936.

Hulnick, Arthur S. "The Intelligence Producer-Policy Consumer Linkage: A Theoretical Approach," *Intelligence and National Security* 1, no. 2 (May 1986): 212–33.

Hunt, David. *Complexity and Planning in the 21st Century: Intelligence Requirements to Unlock the Mystery*. Newport, RI: Naval War College, 2000.

Hunt, Earl, and Franca Agnoli. "The Whorfian Hypothesis. A Cognitive Psychology Perspective," *Psychological Review* 98, no. 3 (1991): 377–89.

Hymes, Dell, ed. *Language in Culture and Society: A Reader in Linguistics and Anthropology*. New York: Harper and Row, 1977.

Iaffaldano, Michelle T., and Paul M. Muchinsky. "Job satisfaction and Job Performance: A Meta-Analysis," *Psychological Bulletin* 97 (1985): 251–73.

James, William. *Principles of Psychology: Volume I*. New York: Dover Press, 1890/1950.

Janis, Irving. *Groupthink*, 2nd ed. Boston: Houghton Mifflin, 1982.

Janssens, Maddy. "Interculture Interaction: A Burden on International Managers?" *Journal of Organizational Behavior* 16 (1995): 155–67.

Jervis, Robert. *Perception and Misperception in International Politics*. Princeton, NJ: Princeton University Press, 1977.

Johnson, David, and Roger Johnson. "The Internal Dynamics of Cooperative Learning Groups" in Richard Slavin, et al., eds. *Learning to Cooperate, Cooperating to Learn*. New York: Plenum, 1985.

———, et al. "Effects of Cooperative, Competitive, and Individualistic Goal Structure on Achievement: A Meta-Analysis," *Psychological Bulletin* 89, no. 1 (1981): 47–62.

———, et al. "The Impact of Positive Goal and Resource Interdependence on Achievement, Interaction, and Attitudes," *Journal of General Psychology* 118, no. 4 (1996): 341–47.

Johnson, Edgar. *Effects of Data Source Reliability on Inference*. Alexandria, VA: Army Research Institute for the Behavioral and Social Sciences, Technical Paper #251, 1974.

Johnston, Rob. *Decision Making and Performance Error in Teams: Research Results*. Arlington, VA: Defense Advanced Research Projects Agency, 1997.

———. "The Effectiveness of Instructional Technology," *Proceedings of the Virtual Reality in Medicine and Developers' Exposition*. Cambridge, MA: VRS, 1995.

———. "Electronic Performance Support Systems and Information Navigation," *Thread* 2, no. 2 (1994): 5–7.

———, and Sunil Bhoyrul. "A Preliminary Report of a Task Analysis of Laparoscopic Cholecystectomy Used to Assess the Effectiveness of a Virtual Reality Surgical Simulator," *Journal of Virtual Reality in Medicine* 2, no. 1 (1996): 16–19.

———, et al. "Assessing a Virtual Reality Surgical Skills Simulator" in Suzanne Weghorst, Hans Sieburg, and Karen Morgan, eds. *Health Care in the Information Age: Future Tools for Transforming Medicine*. Washington, DC: IOS Press, 1996.

———, and J. Dexter Fletcher. *A Meta-Analysis of the Effectiveness of Computer-Based Training for Military Instruction*. Alexandria, VA: Institute for Defense Analyses, 1998.

———, J. Dexter Fletcher, and Sunil Bhoyrul. *The Use of Virtual Reality to Measure Surgical Skill Levels*. Alexandria, VA: Institute for Defense Analyses, 1998.

Jones, Morgan. *The Thinker's Toolkit: 14 Powerful Techniques for Problem Solving*. New York: Times Business, 1998.

Jung, Carl. *The Undiscovered Self*. Translated by R.F.C. Hull. Princeton, NJ: Princeton University Press, 1990.

Kahaner, Larry. *Competitive Intelligence. How to Gather, Analyze, and Use Information to Move Your Business to the Top*. New York: Touchstone, Simon and Schuster, 1996.

Kahneman, Daniel, and Amos Tversky. "Prospect Theory: An Analysis of Decision Under Risk," *Econometrica* 47, no. 2 (1979): 263–91.

―――――, Paul Slovic, and Amos Tversky. *Judgment Under Uncertainty: Heuristics and Biases.* Cambridge: Cambridge University Press, 1982.

Kam, Ephraim. *Surprise Attack. The Victim's Perspective.* Cambridge: Harvard University Press, 1988.

Kaufman, David L., Jr. *Introduction to Systems Thinking.* Minneapolis: Future Systems, 1978.

Kaufman, Roger. "A Holistic Planning Model: A Systems Approach for Improving Organizational Effectiveness and Impact," *Performance and Instruction Journal,* October 1983: 3–10.

Kent, Sherman. *Strategic Intelligence for American World Policy.* Princeton: Princeton University Press, 1966.

―――――. "Words of Estimative Probability," *Sherman Kent and the Board of National Estimates: Collected Essays.* Washington, DC: Center for the Study of Intelligence, 1994.

Kirk, Jerome, and Marc Miller. *Reliability and Validity in Qualitative Research. Qualitative Research Methods, Volume 1.* Newbury Park, CA: Sage, 1986.

Kirkpatrick, Lyman B., Jr. *Captains Without Eyes: Intelligence Failures in World War II.* London: MacMillan Company, 1969.

Klahr, D., and H.A. Simon. "What Have Psychologists (and Others) Discovered About the Process of Scientific Discovery?" *Current Directions in Psychological Science* 10.

Klein, Gary, Roberta Calderwood, and A. Clinton-Cirocco. *Rapid Decision Making on the Fire Ground.* Yellow Springs, OH: Klein Associates, 1985, KA-TR-84-41-7 (prepared under contract MDA903-85-G-0099 for the US Army Research Institute, Alexandria, VA).

Knight, Frank H. *Risk, Uncertainty and Profit.* Boston: Houghton Mifflin, 1921.

Knorr, Klaus. "Foreign Intelligence and the Social Sciences." (Research monograph, Center of International Studies, Princeton University, 1964.)

Krizan, Lisa. *Intelligence Essentials for Everyone.* Washington, DC: Joint Military Intelligence College, 1999.

Krotow, Geraldine. *The Impact of Cognitive Feedback on the Performance of Intelligence Analysts.* Monterey, CA: Naval Postgraduate School, 1992, AD-A252.

Kuhn, Thomas. *The Structure of Scientific Revolutions.* Chicago: The University of Chicago Press, 1970.

Kulik, Chen-Lin, and James Kulik. "Effectiveness of Computer-Based Education in Colleges," *AEDS Journal,* Winter/Spring 1986: 81–108.

————, and Barbara Shwalb, "Effectiveness of Computer-Based Adult Education: A Meta-Analysis," *Journal of Educational Computing Research* 2, no. 2 (1986): 235–52.

Kulik, James. "Meta-Analytic Studies of Findings on Computer-Based Instruction" in Eva Baker and Harold O'Neil, eds. *Technology Assessment in Education and Training*. Hillsdale, NJ: LEA Publishers, 1994.

Lacan, Jacques. *Ecrits*. Translated by Alan Sheridan. New York: W.W. Norton, 1977.

Laqueur, Walter A. *The Uses and Limits of Intelligence*. New Brunswick, NJ: Transaction Publishers, 1993.

Larkin, Jill. "The Role of Problem Representation in Physics" in Debra Gentner and Albert Stevens, eds. *Mental Models*. Hillsdale, NJ: Lawrence Erlbaum Associates, 1983.

Lee, Penny. *The Whorf Theory Complex: A Critical Reconstruction*. Amsterdam: Benjamins, 1996.

Leli, D., and S. Filskov. "Clinical-Actuarial Detection of and Description of Brain Impairment with the Wechsler-Bellevue Form I," *Journal of Clinical Psychology* 37 (1981): 623–29.

Lesgold, Alan, et al. "Expertise in a Complex Skill: Diagnosing X-Ray Pictures" in Michelene Chi, Robert Glaser and Marshall Farr, eds. *The Nature of Expertise*. Hillsdale, NJ: Lawrence Erlbaum Associates, 1988.

Levi-Strauss, Claude. *Structural Anthropology*. New York: The Penguin Press, 1968. (Originally published in 1958.)

Levine, George, ed. *Constructions of the Self*. Brunswick, NJ: Rutgers University Press, 1992.

Levinson, David, and Melvin Ember, eds. *American Immigrant Cultures: Builders of a Nation. Vol. I and II*. New York: Macmillan Reference, 1997.

Litwin, Mark. "How to Measure Survey Reliability and Validity" in Arlene Fink, ed. *The Survey Kit. Volume 7*. Thousand Oaks, CA: Sage, 1995.

Liu, Lisa. "Reasoning Counterfactually in Chinese: Are There Any Obstacles?" *Cognition* 21 (1985): 239–70.

Locke, Edwin A. "The Nature and Causes of Job Satisfaction" in Marvin Dunnette, ed. *Handbook of Industrial and Organizational Psychology*. Chicago: Rand McNally, 1976.

Lockwood, Jonathan, and K. Lockwood. "The Lockwood Analytical Method for Prediction (LAMP)," *Defense Intelligence Journal* 3, no. 2 (1994): 47–74.

Lowenthal, Mark. *Intelligence: From Secrets to Policy*. Washington, DC: CQ, 2000.

Luce, Duncan, and Howard Raiffa. "Utility Theory." Paul Moser, ed. *Rationality in Action. Contemporary Approaches*. New York. Cambridge University Press, 1990.

Lucy, John. *Grammatical Categories and Cognition*. Cambridge: Cambridge University Press, 1992.

———. *Language Diversity and Thought*. Cambridge: Cambridge University Press, 1992.

MacEachin, Douglas J., et al. *The Tradecraft of Analysis: Challenge and Change in the CIA*. Washington, DC: Consortium for the Study of Intelligence, 1994.

Marrin, Stephen. *CIA's Kent School. A Step in the Right Direction*. Paper presented at the International Studies Association Annual Convention, New Orleans, LA, 2002. (http://www.isanet.org/noarchive/marrin.html.)

———. "Improving CIA Analysis by Overcoming Institutional Obstacles" in Russell G. Swenson, ed. *Bringing Intelligence About: Practitioners Reflect on Best Practices*. Washington, DC: Joint Military Intelligence College, 2003.

Mathams, Robert. "The Intelligence Analyst's Notebook" in Douglas Dearth and R. Thomas Goodden, eds. *Strategic Intelligence: Theory and Application*, 2nd ed. Washington, DC: Joint Military Intelligence College, 1995.

Mauss, Marcel. *The Gift: The Form and Reason for Exchange in Archaic Societies*. Translated by W. D. Halls. New York: W. W. Norton, 2000.

Mayo, Elton. *The Human Problems of an Industrial Civilization*. New York: MacMillan, 1933.

McDowell, Don. *Strategic Intelligence: A Handbook for Practitioners, Managers and Users*. Canberra, Australia: Istana Enterprises, 1998.

McEvoy, Glenn M., and Wayne F. Cascio. "Strategies for Reducing Employee Turnover: A Meta-Analysis," *Journal of Applied Psychology* 70, no. 2 (1985): 342–53.

McGuire, Hunter, et al. "Measuring and Managing Quality of Surgery: Statistical vs. Incidental Approaches," *Archives of Surgery* 127 (1992): 733–37.

McKeithen, Katherine, et al. "Knowledge Organization and Skill Differences in Computer Programmers," *Cognitive Psychology* 13 (1981): 307–25.

Mead, George. *Mind, Self, and Society*. Charles Morris, ed. Chicago: University of Chicago Press, 1967.

Meglino, Bruce M., et al. "Effects of Realistic Job Previews: A Comparison Using an Enhancement and a Reduction Preview." *Journal of Applied Psychology* 71 (1988): 259–66.

Meister, David. *Behavioral Analysis and Measurement Methods*. New York: Wiley, 1985.

———. *Human Factors: Theory and Practice*. New York: Wiley, 1971.

Meister, Judith. "Individual Perceptions of Team Learning Experiences Using Video-Based or Virtual Reality Environments," *Dissertation Abstracts International*, UMI No. 9965200, 2000.

Miller, Delbert. *Handbook of Research Design and Social Measurement*. Newbury Park, CA: Sage, 1991.

Miller, George, and Philip Johnson-Laird. *Language and Perception.* Cambridge: Harvard University Press, 1976.

Mills, Theodore. "Power Relations in Three-Person Groups" in Dorwin Cartwright and Alvin Zander, *Group Dynamics: Research and Theory.* New York: Harper & Row, 1960.

Min Qi, *Zhongguo Zhengzhi Wenhua* [Chinese Political Culture]. Kunming, China: Yunnan People's Press, 1989.

Minsky, Marvin, and Seymour Papert. *Artificial Intelligence.* Eugene: Oregon State System of Higher Education, 1974.

Molm, Linda. "Linking Power Structure and Power Use" in Karen Cook, ed. *Social Exchange Theory.* Newbury Park, CA: Sage, 1987.

Moore, David. "Creating Intelligence: Evidence and Inference in the Analysis Process." Unpublished Masters Thesis. Washington, DC: Joint Military Intelligence College, 2002.

Morris, C.D., J.D. Bransford, and J.J. Franks. "Level of Processing Versus Transfer-Appropriate Processing," *Journal of Verbal Learning and Verbal Behavior* 16 (1977).

Morrison, J.E., and J.D. Fletcher. *Cognitive Readiness.* Alexandria, VA: Institute for Defense Analyses, 2001, IDA Paper P-3735.

———, and Larry Meliza. *Foundations of the After-Action Review Process.* Alexandria, VA: Institute for Defense Analyses, 1999.

Mullen, Brian, and Carolyn Copper. "The Relation Between Group Cohesiveness and Performance: An Integration," *Psychological Bulletin,* 115 (1994): 210–27.

National Aeronautics and Space Administration. *Astronaut Fact Book.* NP-2000-09-008JSC. Washington, DC: NASA, 2000.

Neisser, U. *Cognitive Psychology.* New York: Appleton, Century Crofts, 1967.

Nieva, V., E. Fleishman, and A. Rieck. *Team Dimensions: Their Identity, Their Measurement, and Their Relationships,* RN 85-12. Alexandria, VA: US Army Research Institute for the Behavioral and Social Sciences, 1985.

Nijhof, W., and P. Kommers. "An Analysis of Cooperation in Relation to Cognitive Controversy" in Richard Slavin, Shlomo Sharan, Spencer Kagan, et al., eds. *Learning to Cooperate, Cooperating to Learn.* New York: Plenum, 1985.

Nisbett, Richard, and Ara Norenzayan. "Culture and Cognition" in Douglas Medin and Hal Pashler, eds. *Stevens' Handbook of Experimental Psychology,* 3rd ed., New York: John Wiley & Sons, 2002.

Nolte, William. "Preserving Central Intelligence: Assessment and Evaluation in Support of the DCI, " *Studies in Intelligence* 48, no. 3 (2005): 21–25.

Orasanu, Judith. "Shared Mental Models and Crew Performance." Paper presented at the 34th annual meeting of the *Human Factors Society,* Orlando, FL, 1990.

————, and Lynne Martin. "Errors in Aviation Decision Making: A Factor in Accidents and Incidents," *Proceedings of the Working Group on Human Error, Safety, and System Development.* Seattle, WA: International Federation for Information Processing, 1998: 100–107.

Orlansky, Jesse, and Joseph String. *Cost-Effectiveness of Computer-Based Instruction in Military Training.* Alexandria, VA: Institute for Defense Analyses, 1979. IDA P-1375.

————, et al. *The Cost and Effectiveness of the Multi-Service Distributed Training Testbed (MDT2) for Training Close Air Support.* Alexandria, VA: Institute for Defense Analyses, 1997.

————. *The Value of Simulation for Training.* Alexandria, VA: Institute for Defense Analyses, 1994. IDA P-2982.

Paige, Jeffery, and Herbert Simon. "Cognition Processes in Solving Algebra Word Problems" in Benjamin Kleinmuntz, ed. *Problem Solving.* New York: Wiley, 1966.

Patton, Michael. *Qualitative Evaluation and Research Methods,* 2nd ed. Beverly Hills, CA: Sage, 1990.

Perrow, Charles. *Normal Accidents: Living with High Risk Technologies.* Princeton, NJ: Princeton University Press, 1999.

————. Written communications between Perrow and Johnston, 2002.

Peterson, Marilyn. *Applications in Criminal Analysis.* Westport, CT: Greenwood Press, 1995.

————, Bob Morehouse, and Richard Wright, eds. *Intelligence 2000: Revising the Basic Elements.* Sacramento, CA: LEIU and IALEIA, 2000.

Phelps, Ruth, et al. "Effectiveness and Costs of Distance Education Using Computer-Mediated Communication," *American Journal of Distance Education* 5, no. 3 (1991): 7–19.

Pierce, John. "Some Mathematical Methods for Intelligence Analysis," *Studies in Intelligence* 21 (Summer 1977) (declassified): 1–19.

Popper, Karl. *The Logic of Scientific Discovery.* London: Hutchinson, 1959.

————. *Conjectures and Refutations: The Growth of Scientific Knowledge.* New York: Routledge, 2002 reprint.

Porter, Lyman W., Edward E. Lawler, and J. Richard Hackman. *Behavior in Organizations.* New York: McGraw-Hill, 1975.

————, et al. "Organizational Commitment, Job Satisfaction and Turnover Among Psychiatric Technicians," *Journal of Applied Psychology* 59 (1974): 603-609.

Prescott, John, and Stephen Miller, eds. *Proven Strategies in Competitive Intelligence.* New York: John Wiley & Sons, 2001.

Price-Williams, Douglass. *Explorations in Cross-Cultural Psychology.* San Francisco: Chandler and Sharp, 1975.

Putnam, Robert. *Bowling Alone: The Collapse and Revival of American Community.* New York: Simon and Schuster, 2000.

————. "The Prosperous Community: Social Capital and Public Life," *The American Prospect 4, no.* 13 (1993): 35–42.

Quirk, John, et al. *The Central Intelligence Agency: A Photographic History.* Guilford, CT: Foreign Intelligence Press, 1986.

Reason, James. *Human Error.* New York: Cambridge University Press, 1990.

Reichenbach, Hans. *Experience and Prediction.* Chicago: University of Chicago Press, 1938.

Richelson, Jeffrey. *The U.S. Intelligence Community*, 4th ed. Boulder, CO: Westview Press, 1999.

Roethlisberger, Fritz J., and William J. Dickson. *Management and the Worker: An Account of a Research Program Conducted by the Western Electric Company, Hawthorne Works, Chicago.* Boston: Harvard University Press, 1939.

Rosenberg, Marc J. "Performance Technology: Working the System," *Training,* January 1990: 5–10.

Rossi, Peter, and Howard Freeman. *Evaluation. A Systematic Approach,* 5th ed. Newbury Park, CA: Sage, 1993.

Roth, P. L. ,and James E. Campion. "An Analysis of the Predictive Power of the Panel Interview and Pre-Employment Tests," *Journal of Occupational and Organizational Psychology* 65 (1992): 51-60.

Sacks, H. "Promises, Performance, and Principles: An Empirical Study of Parole Decision-Making in Connecticut," *Connecticut Law Review* 9 (1977): 349–422.

Salomon, G., and D.N. Perkins. "Rocky Roads to Transfer: Rethinking Mechanisms of a Neglected Phenomenon," *Educational Psychologist* 24 (1998).

Sapir, Edward. *Language.* New York: Harcourt Brace, 1949.

Sapp, Edwin. "Decision Trees," *Studies in Intelligence* 18 (Winter 1974) (declassified): 45–57.

Sarbin, Theodore. "A Contribution to the Study of Actuarial and Individual Methods of Prediction," *American Journal of Sociology* 48 (1943): 593–602.

Saussure, Ferdinand. *Course in General Linguistics.* Translated by W. Baskin. New York: McGraw-Hill, 1959.

Sawyer, J. "Measurement and Prediction, Clinical and Statistical," *Psychological Bulletin* 66 (1966): 178–200.

Schensul, Jean, and Margaret LeCompte, eds. *Ethnographer's Toolkit. Vol. I–Vol. VII.* Walnut Creek, CA: Alta Mira Press, 1999.

Schofield, W., and J. Garrard. "Longitudinal Study of Medical Students Selected for Admission to Medical School by Actuarial and Committee Methods," *British Journal of Medical Education* 9 (1975): 86–90.

Schum, David. *The Evidential Foundations of Probabilistic Reasoning.* Evanston, IL: Northwestern University Press, 1994.

Scriven, M. "Problems and Prospects for Individualization" in H. Talmage, ed. *Systems of Individualized Education.* Berkley, CA: McCutchan, 1975.

Seashore, S. *Group Cohesiveness in the Industrial Workgroup*. Ann Arbor: University of Michigan Press, 1954.

Segall, Marshall. *Cross-Cultural Psychology: Human Behavior in Global Perspective*. Monterey, CA: Brooks/Cole, 1979.

Senders, John, and Neville Moray. *Human Error: Cause, Prediction and Reduction*. Hillsdale, NJ: Lawrence Earlbaum Associates, 1991.

Shiels, Frederick L. *Preventable Disasters: Why Governments Fail*. Savage, MD: Rowman and Littlefield Publishers, 1991.

Shiffrin, R.M. and W. Schneider. "Controlled and Automatic Human Information Processing: II. Perceptual Learning," *Psychological Review* 84 (1977).

Shlaim, Avi. "Failures in National Intelligence Estimates: The Case of the Yom Kippur War," *World Politics* 28, no. 3 (1976): 348–80.

Shweder, Richard. *Thinking Through Cultures*. Cambridge, MA: Harvard University Press, 1991.

Simmel, Georg. *The Sociology of Georg Simmel*. Translated by K. Wolff. Glencoe, IL: Free Press, 1950.

Simon, D., and Herbert Simon. "Individual Differences in Solving Physics Problems" in Robert Siegler, ed. *Children's Thinking: What Develops?* Hillsdale, NJ: Lawrence Erlbaum Associates, 1978.

Slavin, Robert. "Research on Cooperative Learning: Consensus and Controversy," *Educational Leadership* 47, no. 4 (1989): 52–55.

———. *Cooperative Learning*. New York: Longman, 1983.

Slovic, P., S. Lichtenstein, and B. Fischoff. "Decision-Making" in R.C. Atkinson et al. eds. *Steven's Handbook of Experimental Psychology (2nd ed.), Volume 2: Learning and Cognition*, New York: John Wiley & Sons, 1988.

Solomon, H. *Economic Issues in Cost-Effectiveness Analyses of Military Skill Training*. Alexandria, VA: Institute for Defense Analyses, 1986, IDA P-1897.

Spencer, Herbert. *The Study of Sociology*. New York: D. Appleton. 1874.

Spencer, Ken. "Modes, Media and Methods: The Search for Educational Effectiveness," *British Journal of Educational Technology* 22, no. 1 (1991): 12–22.

Spradley, James. *Participant Observation*. New York: Rinehart and Winston, 1980.

Stanton, Neville, and Sarah Stevenage. "Learning to Predict Human Error: Issues of Acceptability, Reliability and Validity," *Ergonomics*, 41, no. 11 (1998): 1737–56.

Stephenson, William. *The Study of Behavior: Q-Technique and its Methodology*. Chicago: University of Chicago Press, 1953.

Suppes, P., and M. Morningstar. *Computer-Assisted Instruction at Stanford, 1966-68: Data, Models, and Evaluation of the Arithmetic Programs*. New York: Academic Press, 1972.

Thompson, J. R., R. Hopf-Weichel, and R. Geiselman. *The Cognitive Bases of Intelligence Analysis.* Alexandria, VA: Army Research Institute, Research Report 1362, 1984, AD-A146.

Tierney, William G., and Robert A. Rhoads. *Faculty Socialization as Cultural Process: A Mirror of Institutional Commitment.* Washington, DC: ASHE-ERIC Higher Education Report No. 6, 1993.

Tobias, Sigmund. "When Do Instructional Methods Make a Difference?" *Educational Researcher* 11, no. 4 (1982): 4–9.

———, and L. T. Frase. "Educational Psychology and Training" in S. Tobias and J. D. Fletcher, eds. *Training and Retraining: A Handbook for Business, Industry, Government, and the Military.* New York: Macmillan Library Reference, 2001.

Treverton, Gregory F. *Reshaping National Intelligence in an Age of Information.* Cambridge: Cambridge University Press, 2001.

Trier, Jost. *Der deutsche Wortschatz im Sinnbezirk des Verstandes.* Heidelberg: Carl Winter, 1931.

Trochim, William. *The Research Methods Knowledge Base.* Cincinnati, OH: Atomic Dog, 2001.

Tulving, E., and D.M. Thomson. "Encoding Specificity and Retrieval Processes in Episodic Memory," *Psychological Review* 80 (1973).

Tversky, Amos, and Daniel Kahneman. "The Belief in the 'Law of Small Numbers,'" *Psychological Bulletin* 76 (1971): 105–10.

———. "Judgment Under Uncertainty: Heuristics and Biases," *Science* 185 (1974): 1124–31.

US Joint Forces Command. *Department of Defense Dictionary of Military and Associated Terms.* USJFCOM Joint Publication 1-02. Amended through June 5, 2003. (http://www.dtic.mil/doctrine/jel/doddict/index.html.)

von Humboldt, Wilhelm. "Uber die Verschiedenheit des Menschlichen Sprachbaues" in B. Bohr, ed. *Gesammelte Schriften.* Berlin: Verlag, 1907.

Voss, James, and Timothy Post. "On the Solving of Ill-Structured Problems" in Michelene Chi, Robert Glaser and Marshall Farr, eds. *The Nature of Expertise.* Hillsdale, NJ: Lawrence Erlbaum Associates, 1988.

Vygotsky, Lev. *Mind and Society,* Cambridge: Harvard University Press, 1930.

Wanous, John P. *Organizational Entry: Recruitment, Selection, Orientation, and Socialization.* Reading, MA: Addison-Wesley, 1992.

———, et al. "The Effects of Met Expectations on Newcomer Attitudes and Behavior: A Review and Meta-Analysis," *Journal of Applied Psychology* 77 (1992): 288–97.

Warner, Michael. "Wanted: A Definition of 'Intelligence,'" *Studies in Intelligence* 46, no. 3 (2002):15–22.

Weiser, M., and J. Shertz. "Programming Problem Representation in Novice and Expert Programmers," *Instructional Journal of Man-Machine Studies* 14 (1983): 391-96.

Weisgerber, Leo. *Vom Weltbild der Deutschen Sprache.* Dusseldorf: Padago-gischer Verlag Schwann, 1953.

White, Robert. *Task Analysis Methods: Review and Development of Tech-niques for Analyzing Mental Workload in Multiple Task Situations.* St. Louis, MO: McDonnell Douglas Corporation, 1971, MDC J5291.

Whorf, Benjamin. *Language, Thought, and Reality.* New York: John Wiley, 1956.

Wirtz, James J. *The Tet Offensive: Intelligence Failure in War.* Ithaca, NY: Cornell University Press, 1991.

Wisher, R.A., M.A. Sabol, and J.A. Ellis. *Staying Sharp: Retention of Military Knowledge and Skills.* Alexandria, VA: US Army Research Institute for the Behavioral and Social Sciences, 1999, ARI Special Report 39. (<http://www.ari.army.mil>.)

Wohlstetter, Roberta. *Pearl Harbor: Warning and Decision.* Stanford, CA: Stanford University Press, 1962.

Wolf, Eric. *Pathways of Power. Building an Anthropology of the Modern World.* Berkeley: University of California Press, 2001.

Yin, Robert. *Case Study Research: Design and Methods* 2nd ed. Thousand Oaks, CA: Sage, 1994.

Ziemke, Caroline, Philippe Loustaunau, and Amy Alrich. *Strategic Personal-ity and the Effectiveness of Nuclear Deterrence.* Washington, DC: Institute for Defense Analyses, 2000, D-2537.

Zlotnick, Jack. "Bayes' Theorem for Intelligence Analysis" (1972) in H. Bradford Westerfield, ed. *Inside CIA's Private World: Declassified Articles from the Agency's Internal Journal.* New Haven, CT: Yale University Press, 1995.

Zou, Yali, and Enrique Trueba. *Ethnic Identity and Power.* Albany: State University of New York, 1998.

Web resources

Buros Institute of Mental Measurements (http://www.unl.edu/buros/).

Central Intelligence Agency main website (http://www.cia.gov).

Central Intelligence Agency Office of General Council (http://www.cia.gov/ogc/best.htm).

Central Intelligence Agency Officer in Residence Program (http://www.cia.gov//csi/officer.html).

Defense Intelligence Agency (http://www.dia.mil).

Federal Bureau of Investigation (http://www.fbijobs.com or http://www.fbi.gov).

Human Relations Area Files. Yale University. (http://www.yale.edu/hraf/).

National Aeronautics and Space Administration-Johnson Space Center career astronaut biography. (http://www.jsc.nasa.gov/Bios/astrobio_activemgmt.html).

National Imagery and Mapping Agency (http://www.nima.mil/).

National Reconnaissance Office (http://www.nro.gov/).

National Security Agency (http://www.nsa.gov/).

US Air Force (http://aia.lackland.af.mil/aia/).

US Army (http://usaic.hua.army.mil/index.htm).

U.S. Army Center for Army Lessons Learned (http://call.army.mil/).

US Coast Guard (http://www.uscg.mil/USCG.shtm).

US Department of Energy (http://www.energy.gov/engine/content.do).

US Department of Homeland Security (http://www.dhs.gov/dhspublic/).

US Department of State (http://www.state.gov/s/inr/).

US Department of the Treasury (http://www.treasury.gov/).

US Intelligence Community (http://www.intelligence.gov/index.shtml).

US Marine Corps (http://www.usmc.mil/).

US Navy (http://www.nmic.navy.mil/).

AFTERWORD

Joseph Hayes[1]

The unexamined life is not worth living

Socrates.

A very popular error: having the courage of one's convictions; rather, it is a matter of having the courage for an attack on one's convictions!

Nietzsche

Rob Johnston has written a superb book, a study of intelligence as it is actually practiced. Rob's book is alive with specific, practical recommendations about how the practice of intelligence could be made better. The literature of intelligence is overwhelmingly devoted either to studies which, however rigorous in their academic structure, fail to convey the humanness of the enterprise or to books and articles, too often self congratulatory or self promoting, which are little more than assemblages of entertaining anecdotes. Rob's study deserves a place of honor on the very small bookshelf reserved for analytically sound, deeply insightful works on the conduct of intelligence. Any serious discussion of reform or significant change in the ways in which US intelligence is organized, structured, and carried out will need to take this book as a starting point.

Rob's work bears witness to the imagination and commitment to excellence on the part of the senior intelligence officials who made it possible for a cultural anthropologist to carry out his field work in the secret, sometimes hermetically

---

[1] Joseph Hayes is a retired senior officer of the Central Intelligence Agency Directorate of Operations. He served more than 30 years in the clandestine service.

sealed, world of intelligence. Rob's work also bears witness to the tremendous passion among intelligence professionals to understand better what they do, why they do it, and how their work could be improved. There is, in this community, a palpable desire to do better.

Since the tragedy of 9/11 and the bitter controversies surrounding Iraqi WMD, the world of intelligence analysis has been scrutinized with an intensity of almost unprecedented dimensions. The focus of scrutiny, however, has been on the results, not on the process by which the results were produced and certainly not on the largely anonymous corps of civil servants whose work was at the heart of the issue. Those people, and how and why they do what they do, are at the heart of Rob's important study. If we are ever to make the improvements that must be made in the quality of our intelligence work, then we must begin with a more mature and nuanced understanding of who actually does the work, how, and why. There is a context within which the work is done, a definite culture with values, traditions, and procedures that help shape important outcomes.

Rob has characterized a world that I find all too familiar. It is a world in which rewards and incentives are weighted heavily in favor of filling in gaps in conventional knowledge rather than in leading the way to alternative points of view. It is a world in which confirming evidence is welcome and rewarded and disconfirmatory evidence is, at best, unwelcome and, at worst, discounted. It is a world in which the legitimate and often necessary resort to secrecy has served, all too often, to limit debate and discussion. It is a world in which the most fundamentally important questions—what if and why not—are too often seen as distractions and not as invitations to rethink basic premises and assumptions.

Much of the recent discussion concerning the performance of intelligence organizations has been conducted in almost mechanical terms. "Connecting the dots," "mining the nuggets" are phrases offered as a way of understanding the exquisitely subtle, complex business of making intelligence judgments. As Rob Johnston's book makes abundantly clear, this is first and foremost a human enterprise. All of the intellectual power, biases, and paradigms that inform the thinking of the people who actually do the work need to be understood in the organizational context in which they do their work. In the finest tradition of anthropological field research, Rob has observed, collected data rigorously, reflected with deep insight upon it, and produced a study both sophisticated and extremely useful.

I worked myself for more than 30 years in the clandestine operations area of CIA, a part of the Intelligence Community that calls out for the same kind of understanding, professional, and constructive scrutiny this book has devoted to the analytic realm. My fervent hope is that the human intelligence service will benefit from the same kind of rigor and constructive understanding the analytic side has now experienced. My real hope is that Rob is available for the job.

The Author

Dr. Rob Johnston is an ethnographer who specializes in the cultural anthropology of work. He has been a research staff member at the Institute for Defense Analyses and a Director of Central Intelligence Postdoctoral Research Fellow at the Central Intelligence Agency's Center for the Study of Intelligence, where he is now a member of the staff.

Dr. Johnston is a Fellow of the Royal Anthropological Institute, the Society for Applied Anthropology, and the Inter-University Seminar on Armed Forces and Society.